I0435062

# South Carolina's
## Forests, 2006

Roger C. Conner, Tim O. Adams,
Tony G. Johnson, and Sonja N. Oswalt

United States
Department of
Agriculture

Forest Service

Southern
Research Station

Resource Bulletin
SRS-158

Roger C. Conner is a Research Forester with the U.S. Department of Agriculture Forest Service, Southern Research Station, Forest Inventory and Analysis Research Work Unit, Knoxville, TN 37919.

Tim O. Adams is the Resource Development Division Director with the South Carolina Forestry Commission, Columbia, SC 29212.

Tony G. Johnson is a Resource Analyst with the U.S. Department of Agriculture Forest Service, Southern Research Station, Forest Inventory and Analysis Research Work Unit, Knoxville, TN 37919.

Sonja N. Oswalt is a Forester with the U.S. Department of Agriculture Forest Service, Southern Research Station, Forest Inventory and Analysis Research Work Unit, Knoxville, TN 37919.

Photos by Michelle Johnson unless otherwise noted.

Front cover: top left, cypress at Woods Bay State Natural Area, a large Carolina Bay in coastal South Carolina; top right, hiking path in the Harbison State Forest; bottom, planted longeaf pine on previous farmland in Sumter County. Back cover: top left, planted pine stand in Sumter County; top right, cypress at Woods Bay State Natural Area, a large Carolina Bay in coastal South Carolina; bottom, Table Rock watershed in Pickens County.

Table Rock Mountain in Pickens County.

# South Carolina's
## Forests, 2006

Roger C. Conner, Tim O. Adams,
Tony G. Johnson, and Sonja N. Oswalt

Harbison State Forest provides outdoor recreational opportunties for Midland residents.

*Henry E. Kodama*

*Jimmy L. Reaves*

Welcome to the most recent Forest Inventory Analysis (FIA) report. Within these pages you'll find exhaustive information about the status of South Carolina's forest resource, from the number of trees and volume of wood currently growing in our State, to forest composition and stand structure, to identification of land ownership. Never before has this information been more critical to the quality of life, resource planning, and economic well being of our State.

Data from an ongoing study of the impact of the forest and agricultural industries show that forestry has emerged as the number one manufacturing industry in the State with regard to employment and wages. Forestry provides 44,708 jobs in the Palmetto State with an annual labor income of $2.4 billion. Overall, forestry contributes nearly $17.5 billion annually to South Carolina's economy. These numbers confirm forestry's role as a primary economic driver.

We know that forestry's economic impact has expanded in recent years. As a result of research contained in this report, we also know that South Carolina has more standing timber volume now than ever recorded, that growth exceeds harvests, and total forest area has remained stable at more than 12 million acres. So, we can be confident that the resource will be there to support the industry and the economy into the future. Most importantly, our forests can support expanding industry investments while still providing clean watersheds, beautiful landscapes, and abundant wildlife.

The U.S. Forest Service completed the first inventory of the Nation's forests in the 1930s. In the 1990s, recognizing the importance of high yield forests in all of the Southern States, southern forestry agencies and the U.S. Forest Service began working together to reduce the interval between inventories. South Carolina's 2001 report was the first to be published under the enhanced FIA program. "The State of South Carolina's Forests, 2006" is our second report and one of the first in the South to publish data summaries from the complete remeasurement of the State's annual inventory locations. Valuable additions to this year's report include comprehensive information about forestry's contribution to South Carolina's economy and forest health subjects such as a survey of invasive plants.

The South Carolina Forestry Commission looks forward to continuing our productive partnership with the U.S. Forest Service and to further emphasizing the relevance of forestry in the 21st century through the FIA program.

*Henry E. Kodama*
*South Carolina State Forester*
*South Carolina Forestry Commission*

*Jimmy L. Reaves*
*Director, Southern Research Station,*
*U.S. Forest Service*

The Forest and Rangeland Renewable Resources Research Act of 1978 authorized surveys of our Nation's forest resources. These surveys are part of a continuing, nationwide undertaking by the regional experiment stations of the U.S. Department of Agriculture Forest Service. Inventories of the 13 Southern States (Alabama, Arkansas, Florida, Georgia, Kentucky, Louisiana, Mississippi, North Carolina, Oklahoma, South Carolina, Tennessee, Texas, and Virginia) the Commonwealth of Puerto Rico, and the Virgin Islands are conducted by the Southern Research Station, Forest Inventory and Analysis (FIA) Research Work Unit, operating from its headquarters in Knoxville, TN, and offices in Asheville, NC, and Starkville, MS. The primary objective of these appraisals is to develop and maintain the resource information needed to formulate sound forest policies and programs.

Additional information about any aspect of this survey may be obtained from:

Forest Inventory and Analysis
Southern Research Station
4700 Old Kingston Pike
Knoxville, TN 37919

Telephone: 865-862-2000

This resource bulletin highlights changes in South Carolina's forest resources as interpreted from the second cycle of annual measurements. Annual surveys of U.S. forests were originally mandated by the Agricultural Research Extension and Education Reform Act of 1998 (Farm Bill). They feature: (1) a nationally consistent, fixed-radius, four-point plot configuration; (2) a systematic national sampling design consisting of a base grid derived by subdividing the Environmental Monitoring and Assessment Program grid into roughly 6,000-acre hexagons; (3) integration of the forest inventory and forest health monitoring sampling designs; (4) annual measurement of a fixed proportion of permanent plots; (5) reporting of data or data summaries within 6 months after yearly sampling; (6) a default 5-year moving average estimator, with provisions for optional estimators based on techniques for updating information; and (7) a summary report every 5 years.

Additional information about annual surveys is available at http://fia.fs.fed.us/.

The Southern Research Station's Forest Inventory and Analysis (FIA) Research Work Unit and the South Carolina Forestry Commission began data collection for this ninth survey of South Carolina in 2001. The strategy involves rotating measurements of five systematic samples (or panels), each of which represents about 20 percent of all plots in the State. The 20-percent systematic sample is referred to as one panel of inventory data. A panel may take more than or less than 1 year to complete. This bulletin provides inventory statistics and discusses the principal findings from the full remeasurement of all five panels of annual inventory data from the mapped-plot design. Forest land estimates and inventory volume, growth, removals, and mortality statistics are summarized from the data collected for the five panels.

Eight previous periodic inventories completed in 1936, 1947, 1958, 1968, 1978, 1986, 1993, and 2001 provide statistics for measuring changes and trends at the State level. However, caution is advised when making comparisons at the sub-State level. The annual system represents a dramatic departure from methods used to conduct the previous periodic surveys. Moreover, the annual system continues to evolve as changing technologies are adapted and implemented to improve FIA surveys. The 2006 inventory, for instance, incorporates land area stratification estimates (see Current phase 1—land area stratification in Appendix A—Inventory Methods) based on National Land Cover Data satellite imagery which replaces the aerial photography estimation method used in previous inventories. Improving the accuracy or efficiency of the FIA surveys is justification for altering how the inventory is conducted. However, change detection and trend analysis over time become more difficult due to differences in inventory methods.

The 2006 inventory data, as well as data for other States and survey years, are available at http://www.ncrs2.fs.fed.us/4801/fiadb/fim30/wcfim30.asp. Tabular summaries of the current resource statistics for South Carolina used in this report are available at http://srsfia2.fs.fed.us/states/south_carolina.shtml. Click on the 2006 survey year. Tabular data for previous surveys also are available at that Web site.

## Acknowledgments

We gratefully acknowledge the South Carolina Forestry Commission (SCFC) for its role in collecting the field data. The following SCFC and Southern Research Station, Forest Inventory and Analysis (SRS-FIA) field personnel contributed to the inventory effort:

**SCFC**
Chisolm Beckham
Russell Bedenbaugh
Wesley Bouknight
Alan Bowen
Woodrow Cox, III
Brandon Craig
Brant Elliott
Barry Farrell
Ryan McCracken
Doug Mills
Christina Mitchell
Herbert Nicholson
Stephen Patterson
Austin Powell
Jeff Riggin
Byron Rominger, Coordinator
Gretchen Spaulding
Holly Welch
Eric West

**SRS-FIA**
Linda Burke, QA/QC
Chad Clark
David Crawford
Joseph DiModica
Phillip Fry
Jeremy Grayson
Keith Gustafson
Mike Maki
Russ Oaks
Matthew Powell
Lucas Recore
Jason Renchy
Jeremy Rogers, QA/QC
Justin Seaborne
Warren Tucker

We appreciate the cooperation of other public agencies and private landowners in providing access to measurement plots. We also would like to thank Brett Butler, Research Forester with the Northern Research Station for providing the data from the National Woodland Owner Survey of South Carolina.

# Contents

# Contents

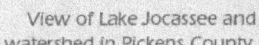
View of Lake Jocassee and watershed in Pickens County.

View of Lake Jocassee in Pickens County.

## Highlights from the Ninth Forest Inventory of South Carolina

### Area

• Total forest area has remained relatively stable over time, and amounted to 12.9 million acres in 2006. Forests occupy 67 percent of the land area of South Carolina.

• Timberland area now totals > 12.8 million acres, up 5 percent from 2001. Hardwood timber types occupy nearly 6.8 million acres (54 percent) of timberland, an increase of 9 percent during the past 5 years.

• Softwood forest types occupy 5.9 million acres, or 46 percent of the State's timberland area. Area of planted pine remains statistically unchanged at about 3.1 million acres.

• Loblolly-shortleaf pine is the predominant forest-type group and occupies 5.3 million acres.

### Ownership

• Most (59 percent) of the State's 12.9 million acres of forest land is owned by private individuals. Forest industry owns 11 percent, down from 16 percent in 2001. Corporate ownership has risen from 16 percent in 2001 to 18 percent as of 2006.

• Nearly 7.3 million acres of South Carolina's private forest land is in the hands of some 262,000 private individuals. One-fifth (21 percent) of these family forest landowners ranked the production of timber products as an important management objective.

### Volume

• As of 2006, total all live volume on timberland in South Carolina amounted to 21.5 billion cubic feet; the most volume ever reported for the State.

• All live volume is split almost evenly between softwoods (10.6 billion cubic feet) and hardwoods (10.9 billion cubic feet). The loblolly-shortleaf pine species group accounted for 8.8 billion cubic feet (83 percent) of the all live softwood volume.

### Net Growth and Removals

• Total net annual growth of all live trees on timberland averaged > 1.2 billion cubic feet per year between 2002 and 2006.

• Net growth for all live softwood trees on timberland averaged 817.0 million cubic feet per year, and removals averaged 596.1 million cubic feet per year. Planted pine stands account for 493 million cubic feet (41 percent) of total net annual growth, and 314 million cubic feet (39 percent) of total annual removals.

• Hardwoods are growing wood at a rate of 387.3 million cubic feet per year, an increase of 27 percent over the record-setting mark of 305.9 million cubic feet per year set during the previous survey. Hardwood removals dropped from an average of 250.7 million cubic feet per year between 1994 and 2001 to the current 217.7 million cubic feet per year.

Waterfall in Oconee County.

## Economic Impact

• Forestry is as important to South Carolina as it has ever been, contributing $17.45 billion annually to the State's economy and providing support for almost 45,000 families.

• In South Carolina, forestry has emerged as the leading manufacturing industry in terms of employment and labor income. Nearly 45,000 people, earning $2.43 billion in labor income, are directly employed in the forestry sector as defined by a 2006 economic Impact Analysis for Planning (IMPLAN) analysis.

• The export of South Carolina forest products approached $1 billion in annual value in 2006 (South Carolina Forestry Commission 2007). Aided by the declining value of U.S. currency in the world market, the value of South Carolina's forest products export grew 59 percent, from $604 million in 2001 to >$962 million in 2006.

• There were about 75 sawmills, pulpwood mills, and other primary wood-processing plants operating in South Carolina in 2005. These mills averaged nearly 755 million cubic feet of timber products per year (including domestic fuelwood and plant byproducts) between 2001 and 2005.

• Average annual output of roundwood products (including domestic fuelwood) declined from 673 million cubic feet in the previous survey period, to an average of 669 million cubic feet between 2001 and 2005.

• Roundwood harvested for saw log and pulpwood production amounted to 260 and 311 million cubic feet, respectively. These two products accounted for 85 percent of the total roundwood production for the State.

## Forest Health

• Total mortality of live trees on South Carolina's forest land averaged 199.6 million cubic feet per year between 2002 and 2006, totaling 998.0 million cubic feet for the period. The current mortality was split almost equally between softwood (54 percent) and hardwood (46 percent) species.

• Redbay trees in some eastern counties of South Carolina, Georgia, and Florida are showing symptoms of Laurel wilt disease. However, FIA surveys have not yet detected a substantial increase in redbay mortality in South Carolina.

• Japanese honeysuckle (*Lonicera japonica*) was the most frequently observed nonnative invasive plant species in South Carolina, followed by Chinese/European privet species (*Ligustrum sinense, L. vulgare*). The most frequently observed nonnative invasive tree species was Chinese tallowtree (*Triadica sebifera*).

Diverse forest types at Piedmont Forestry Center in Pickens County.

Cypress at Woods Bay State Natural Area, a large Carolina Bay in coastal South Carolina.

## Overview

There are forces at work that affect the forest extent, condition, and health. Surveys conducted by Forest Inventory and Analysis (FIA) provide data useful in evaluating the distribution, character, and health of forest resources at the State level. Forest health can be broadly gauged by determining the intensity and cause of tree mortality, or by evaluating the current status of one or more forest health indicators. Some understanding of current forest conditions can be gained by analyzing past changes in forest structure brought about by natural forces, or from forest management activities. Human influences on forests can be gauged by noting trends in forest land ownership, analyzing changes in land use, and tracking changing landowner priorities and values attributed to owning forest land. Quantifying the importance of forest resources to a State's economy depends on timely and accurate assessments of forest extent and condition.

This report provides a general assessment of South Carolina's forest resources, with particular focus on the economic values that forests provide. The descriptive analysis presented here can serve as a starting point for detailed analyses of specific forest resource issues.

### A New Way to Monitor Forest Resources—Remeasurement of the Annual Inventory

The 2001 FIA report for South Carolina (Conner and others 2004) was the first in the South to publish statewide forest resource estimates based on the newly implemented annual inventory system. A principal advantage to adopting the annual inventory methodology, as was noted in the 2001 report, is the improved timeliness for updating forest resource estimates.

An analytical inconvenience accompanying the change in inventory methods is the loss of the ability to directly compare current and previous resource estimates, or track resource trends established by the periodic inventories. Change detection is confounded by sampling "noise" introduced with any new sampling methodology. Comparisons to past data made in this report are offered with the understanding that changes noted in resource estimates over time are due to both measured differences and differences introduced as a result of altering inventory methods.

Planted pine stand in Sumter County.

## Forces of Change: Ownership and Land Use Patterns

Changes in land use and ownership are two primary forces of change that work directly to influence the extent and condition of South Carolina's forest land. Change in forest land ownership often brings with it a change in the reasons for owning the land. Having knowledge about forest landowner intent is essential to assessing the impact the landowner might have on the management and availability of the State's forests. Traditional timber harvesting or other forest product-based uses may be replaced by desires to develop and manage habitat for wildlife or provide new recreational opportunity. Change in ownership also can lead to a change in land use, particularly if there are plans to develop the land. Loss of forest land to urbanization continues to be a concern. However, the rate of conversion to development seems to have slowed recently, perhaps in response to the recent economic downturn.

The 2000 Census (U.S. Department of Commerce 2000) reports the population in South Carolina at just over 4.0 million individuals, or about 133 people per square mile of land. Since the 1990 census, an additional 525,000 people now make their home in the State. Increased population can bring increased pressure on limited natural resources, including the State's forest land.

Table 1 summarizes the distribution of land by use in South Carolina since 1968. Some general trends are apparent. Total area of South Carolina is nearly 20.5 million acres, including 1.2 million acres of census water and nearly 127,000 acres of noncensus water. Forests occupy almost 67 percent of the State's land area, or about 12.9 million acres. The remaining 6.3 million acres of land reflect a variety of nonforest uses such as agriculture and urban development. Total nonforest land has declined by one-half million acres since 2001. Land used for agriculture has declined by 60 percent since 1968. Cropland has declined by one-half over the past nearly 40 years and is

Longleaf pine stand established in former pasture in Barnwell County.

2

Table 1—Total land and water area in South Carolina by land use and survey year

| Land use | Year | | | | | |
|---|---|---|---|---|---|---|
| | 1968 | 1978 | 1986 | 1993 | 2001 | 2006 |
| | | | *acres* | | | |
| **Forest land** | | | | | | |
| Timberland | 12,426,584 | 12,502,906 | 12,178,756 | 12,454,925 | 12,221,404 | 12,800,645 |
| Productive reserved | 70,500 | 72,399 | 78,216 | 190,632 | 194,081 | 86,855 |
| Other forest land | 12,655 | 3,893 | — | — | — | 6,620 |
| Total | 12,509,739 | 12,579,198 | 12,256,972 | 12,645,557 | 12,415,485 | 12,894,120 |
| **Nonforest land** | | | | | | |
| Agriculture | | | | | | |
| Cropland | 3,178,098 | 3,296,240 | 3,185,044 | 2,607,357 | 2,188,940 | 1,597,901 |
| Pasture | 1,029,342 | 1,006,997 | 898,212 | 875,214 | 826,881 | 957,334 |
| Idle | 854,039 | 310,717 | 388,058 | 443,883 | 482,652 | 451,899 |
| Other farm[a] | 164,915 | 208,414 | 150,617 | 131,864 | 61,038 | 165,170 |
| Total agriculture land | 5,226,394 | 4,822,368 | 4,621,931 | 4,058,318 | 3,559,511 | 3,172,304 |
| Urban and other | 962,901 | 1,206,634 | 1,661,884 | 1,976,857 | 2,611,513 | 2,481,512 |
| Marsh | 489,164 | 511,199 | 525,867 | 544,228 | 586,509 | 597,945 |
| Total nonforest land | 6,678,459 | 6,540,201 | 6,809,682 | 6,579,403 | 6,757,533 | 6,251,761 |
| **Water** | | | | | | |
| Noncensus | 191,660 | 230,308 | 253,898 | 37,424 | 89,365 | 126,958 |
| Census | 509,216 | 525,493 | 591,667 | 1,222,167 | 1,222,160 | 1,222,110 |
| Total water | 700,876 | 755,801 | 845,565 | 1,259,591 | 1,311,525 | 1,349,068 |
| Total land and water area[b] | 19,889,074 | 19,875,200 | 19,912,219 | 20,484,551 | 20,484,543 | 20,494,949 |
| Total land area[c] | 19,379,858 | 19,349,707 | 19,320,552 | 19,262,384 | 19,262,383 | 19,272,839 |

— = no sample for the cell.
[a] Includes orchards and wildlife openings.
[b] U.S. Bureau of the Census.
[c] Excludes census water.

down nearly 600,000 acres in the past 5 years alone. Another long-term trend in land use is the increase in urbanized areas which have risen from < 1 million acres in 1968 to nearly 2.5 million acres in 2006. Tracking these two trends is important because shifts in agriculture and urban land uses often have a direct impact on the extent and condition of South Carolina's forest land.

Clearing land for agriculture was once the primary reason for loss of forest. Although conversions to agriculture still occur, the principal threat to loss of forest land since the late 1970s has been urbanization. Table 1 shows that land classified as urban and other declined slightly since 2001, indicating that some acres previously converted to a nonforest land use may have been planted or have reverted naturally to a forested condition. Whereas most of the loss of forest land due to urbanization

is permanent, clearing of forest land for crops or pasture, in many instances, can be reversed. In fact, idle cropland and pasture continue to be the primary source for new acres of forest land, either from planting or from natural reversion.

## Who Owns South Carolina's Forest Land?

Changes in ownership can affect how forest land is managed. FIA classifies land ownership broadly as either private or public. The private owner category is subdivided into individuals, forest industry, and corporate owners. Public forest land includes national forests, other Federal lands, and State, county, and municipal ownership classes. Figure 1 shows the percent distribution of South Carolina's forest land as of 2006. As is typically the case, most (59 percent) of the State's 12.9 million acres of forest land is owned by private individuals. Forest industry now controls just 11 percent, down from 16 percent in 2001. Corporate ownership has risen from 16 percent in 2001 to 18 percent

as of 2006. These changes may appear slight in magnitude but they tend to mask the degree to which changes in ownership are altering the face of forestry in South Carolina and throughout the southern region, as well.

Millions of acres of South Carolina's timberland have changed hands over the past 2 decades, particularly acres once belonging to forest industry. The beginning of forest industry's divestiture of its timberland was first noted in the 1993 report on South Carolina's forests (Conner 1998). The downward trend in industry-owned forest acres has continued. As of 2006, forest industry owned 1.4 million acres, which is 575,000 fewer acres than were under industry management just 5 years ago and 1.2 million fewer acres than the 2.6 million reported in 1986—the peak of industry-owned timberland in South Carolina. Some of these former forest industry acres are now owned by private individuals, while others are now under corporate ownership.

Corporate timberland amounted to >2.3 million acres in 2006, up from 1.9 million in 2001. These timberland acres are largely held in timber investment and management organizations, real estate investment trusts, limited liability corporations, and similar organizations. As forest industry-owned and managed timberland acres, there was some assurance that they would remain in the timber base and contribute to the State's wood supply. However, new landowners may have other management goals and priorities in mind. Future surveys will continue to track changes in forest land ownership and assess the impact these changes have on the use and management of South Carolina's timberlands.

Total forest land: 12.9 million acres

Figure 1—Percent forest land area by owner, South Carolina, 2006.

4

## Family Forest Landowners—Shaping South Carolina's Private Forests

The care and management of nearly 7.3 million acres of South Carolina's private forest land is in the hands of some 262,000 individuals (table 2). Predicting what these family forest landowners intend to do with their land is difficult without some knowledge of their interests and ownership objectives. The National Woodland Owner Survey (Butler 2008) gathers statistics describing the characteristics of these family forest owners and the land they own. This information provides some insight as to how they might manage and use their forest lands in the years to come.

The size of a forested tract often dictates how, or if, that particular forest parcel will be managed. The rule-of-thumb is that it is not financially viable to manage for timber products on parcels <10 acres in size. In South Carolina, <6 percent (413,000 acres) of the family forest land is in tracts ranging from 1 to 9 acres (table 2). Family forest

**Table 2—Area and number of family-owned forests in South Carolina by size of forest landholdings, 2006**

| Size of forest landholdings | Area | | Owners | |
| acres | Acres<br>*thousand* | SE<br>*percent* | Number<br>*thousand* | SE<br>*percent* |
|---|---|---|---|---|
| 1–9 | 413 | 38.7 | 158 | 20.9 |
| 10–19 | 425 | 37.7 | 33 | 16.5 |
| 20–49 | 1,030 | 17.1 | 36 | 10.4 |
| 50–99 | 1,114 | 16.0 | 18 | 11.5 |
| 100–199 | 1,203 | 15.0 | 10 | 12.1 |
| 200–499 | 1,483 | 12.5 | 5 | 9.1 |
| 500–999 | 706 | 23.9 | 1 | 15.2 |
| 1,000–4,999 | 777 | 21.9 | 1 | 14.0 |
| 5,000–9,999 | 91 | 163.8 | <1 | 37.9 |
| 10,000+ | 58 | 205.2 | <1 | 46.0 |
| Total | 7,300 | 2.0 | 262 | 12.6 |

SE = sampling error.

Demand for outdoor recreational opportunities influence management of public and private forest land. (Long Shoals Wayside Park)

landholdings in tracts from 20 acres to < 500 acres in size amount to > 4.8 million acres. Another 1.6 million family forest acres are in tracts at least 500 acres in size, including 149,000 acres in tracts > 5,000 acres.

Based on size of landholdings alone, the majority of South Carolina's family forest land offers potential for a variety of management opportunities. Many of these landowners realize the financial potential their land holds. Land investment was ranked as important or very important by some 136,000 family forest owners (52 percent), potentially affecting about 4.5 million acres (table 3). Some 55,000 landowners (21 percent) ranked the production of timber products as an important objective, while nearly one-quarter (23 percent) of family forest owners considered production of firewood

or biofuel an important use of their forest land. Recent activity on some of these privately owned acres provides evidence of landowners taking advantage of the opportunities that owning forest land offers. In the past 5 years, about 3.3 million acres have undergone a timber harvest, another 2.3 million have been site prepped for planting, and 2.8 million acres have been planted (table 4).

The production of forest products for financial gain, however, is not always the primary motivation for owning forest land. Sixty-five percent of family forest owners, holding nearly 5.1 million acres, ranked passing the land on to their children as an important incentive (table 3). Aesthetics (73 percent of family forest landowners), privacy (66 percent), and protecting nature

**Table 3—Area and number of family-owned forests in South Carolina by reason for owning forest land, 2006**

| Reason[a] | Area | | Owners | |
|---|---|---|---|---|
| | Acres | SE | Number | SE |
| | thousand | percent | thousand | percent |
| To enjoy beauty or scenery | 4,456 | 4.5 | 192 | 16.0 |
| To protect nature and biologic diversity | 3,501 | 5.9 | 116 | 20.3 |
| For land investment | 4,479 | 4.5 | 136 | 18.5 |
| Part of home or vacation home | 3,260 | 6.7 | 156 | 19.5 |
| Part of farm or ranch | 2,692 | 8.0 | 65 | 25.6 |
| Privacy | 3,654 | 5.6 | 173 | 17.1 |
| To pass land on to children or other heirs | 5,060 | 3.9 | 169 | 17.2 |
| To cultivate/collect nontimber forest products | 816 | 21.0 | 25 | 46.8 |
| For production of firewood or biofuel | 623 | 26.6 | 59 | 39.5 |
| For production of saw logs, pulpwood or other timber products | 3,905 | 5.2 | 55 | 22.0 |
| Hunting or fishing | 3,087 | 6.6 | 70 | 27.7 |
| For recreation other than hunting or fishing | 1,934 | 10.0 | 32 | 16.3 |
| No answer | 48 | 262.9 | 1 | 88.6 |

SE = sampling error.

Numbers include landowners who ranked each objective as very important (1) or important (2) on a seven-point Likert scale.

[a] Categories are not exclusive.

Table 4—Area and number of family-owned forests in South Carolina by recent (past 5 years) forestry activity, 2006

| Activity[a] | Area | | Owners | |
|---|---|---|---|---|
| | Acres | SE | Number | SE |
| | thousand | percent | thousand | percent |
| Timber harvest | 3,303 | 6.5 | 33 | 11.8 |
| Collection of NTFPs | 419 | 38.8 | 9 | 34.1 |
| Site preparation | 2,349 | 8.4 | 25 | 50.4 |
| Tree planting | 2,816 | 7.2 | 34 | 37.6 |
| Fire hazard reduction | 1,885 | 10.1 | 34 | 40.3 |
| Application of chemicals | 1,475 | 12.6 | 10 | 26.0 |
| Road/trail maintenance | 2,291 | 8.6 | 22 | 29.6 |
| Wildlife habitat improvement | 1,562 | 12.0 | 9 | 15.9 |
| Posting land | 3,022 | 7.2 | 56 | 38.1 |
| Private recreation | 3,499 | 6.3 | 71 | 31.5 |
| Public recreation | 523 | 32.3 | 6 | 31.0 |
| None of the above | 1,377 | 13.6 | 104 | 16.8 |

SE = sampling error; NTFPs = nontimber forest products.
[a] Categories are not exclusive.

and biodiversity (44 percent) were also highly valued benefits of possessing forest land. One-fourth of the landowners hold forest land as part of their farm or ranch, likely living within close proximity. These importance rankings reflect the personal and physical attachment family forest owners have with their land. Although these reasons for owning forest land are not necessarily income producing, they can be compatible with landowners' desires to manage and financially benefit from their land. The fact that landowners understand both personal and financial objectives can be accomplished through wise management

Nearly one-third of all family forest landowners list hunting as a primary reason for owning forest land.

bodes well for the long-term care and sustainable use of a large portion of South Carolina's private forests.

Knowing what family forest landowners potentially have planned for their land over the next 5 years adds to that positive outlook for the long term. Some 48,000 owners with nearly 2.4 million forested acres plan to at least maintain their land as forest while 13,000 owners with 1.3 million acres already in their possession said they have plans to buy additional forest land (table 5). Plans for others (6,000 owners) include converting some of the nonforest land in their possession to forest. With regards to continued timber supply, about 17,000 family forest owners plan to harvest saw logs or pulpwood from their 2.5 million acres of forest land.

Some landowner plans, however, may not result in positive outcomes for the State's private forest land. About 18,000 landowners revealed plans to sell some or all of the combined 612,000 acres of forest land they own (table 5). Changes in ownership usually raise concerns about whether the land will continue to be maintained as forest. Other concerns might arise from plans to subdivide some or all of their forest land (8,000 owners with 173,000 acres), or convert it to a nonforest land use (6,000 owners with 313,000 acres).

**Table 5—Area and number of family-owned forests in South Carolina by landowners' future (next 5 years) plans for their forest land, 2006**

| Future plans[a] | Area | | Owners | |
|---|---|---|---|---|
| | Acres | SE | Number | SE |
| | *thousand* | *percent* | *thousand* | *percent* |
| Leave it as is—no activity | 1,105 | 16.6 | 90 | 23.6 |
| Minimal activity to maintain forest land | 2,385 | 8.7 | 48 | 18.6 |
| Harvest firewood | 857 | 20.1 | 23 | 49.9 |
| Harvest saw logs or pulpwood | 2,525 | 7.9 | 17 | 18.1 |
| Collect nontimber forest products | 256 | 61.0 | 4 | 29.9 |
| Sell some or all of their forest land | 612 | 27.1 | 18 | 31.0 |
| Give some or all of their forest land to heirs | 1,763 | 10.8 | 65 | 28.0 |
| Subdivide some or all of their forest land and sell subdivisions | 173 | 87.5 | 8 | 61.9 |
| Buy more forest land | 1,341 | 13.7 | 13 | 27.6 |
| Convert some or all of their forest land to another use | 313 | 49.9 | 6 | 48.9 |
| Convert another land use to forest land | 418 | 38.2 | 6 | 33.1 |
| No current plans | 743 | 23.3 | 40 | 23.6 |
| Unknown | 228 | 69.6 | 26 | 70.8 |
| Other | 201 | 75.6 | 6 | 49.8 |
| No answer | 191 | 80.5 | 7 | 39.2 |

SE = sampling error.

[a] Categories are not exclusive.

## Forest Cover

The nearly 12.9 million acres of forest land in South Carolina in 2006 represents the high mark for estimates of forest land in the State. Forest area is split between hardwoods (6.9 million acres) and softwoods (5.9 million acres). The current estimate of forest land includes almost 87,000 acres of reserved land. These are restricted-use areas including national or State parks, monuments, wildlife refuges, recreation sites, or other similarly protected areas where timber harvesting is severely limited or prohibited. The current area of reserved forest land is 107,000 fewer acres than were reported in 2001. Some of the decline is due to reclassification of reserved acres to timberland as a result of improved ownership identification.

The 2006 estimate of forest land is nearly 479,000 acres or 4 percent more than was reported in 2001. The increase in forest land occurred in all parts of the State but was greatest in the Northern Coastal Plain survey unit (see fig. A.1 for map of survey units). There, forest land increased by 248,000 acres or 5 percent since 2001. Forest land in the Piedmont increased 4 percent, or 175,000 acres:

| Survey unit | Forest land | | |
| --- | --- | --- | --- |
| | 2001 | 2006 | Change |
| | *thousand acres* | | |
| Southern Coastal Plain | 3,324.8 | 3,380.4 | +55.6 |
| Northern Coastal Plain | 4,628.9 | 4,876.8 | +247.9 |
| Piedmont | 4,461.8 | 4,636.8 | +175.0 |
| Total | 12,415.5 | 12,894.0 | +478.5 |

Some of the increase in forest land in each unit is the result of natural regeneration or planting on what was previously nonforest land. However, the sampling methods for the 2006 inventory were altered to improve forest area estimation, and as a result, a portion of these additional acres of forest land were likely already established but were sampled for the first time during the 2006 survey. An attempt to identify how the new methods contributed to the increase in forest land, specifically the increase in timberland area, is discussed below. In addition, a small-scale study was conducted in 2007 by the South Carolina Forestry Commission to address questions about changes in survey methods and the increase in forest area. See "Pee Dee region special study: an independent estimate of forest area in five coastal counties" (see sidebar, next page) for a summary of their findings.

Hiking path in the Harbison State Forest.

# Pee Dee Region Special Study: An Independent Estimate of Forest Area in Five Coastal Counties

A special study was conducted by South Carolina Forestry Commission-Forest Inventory and Analysis (SCFC-FIA) crews to answer questions concerning the forest area estimates from the 2006 FIA survey which showed a 479,000-acre increase in forest land, statewide. Over one-half of this increase occurred in five counties (Berkeley, Florence, Georgetown, Marion, and Williamsburg Counties) of the Pee Dee region of South Carolina. With recent increases in population, the common perception was that rural forest lands were on the decline due to development pressure.

Traditionally, FIA determined forest area based on interpretations of sample points on aerial photography with field verification. FIA transitioned to stratified sampling for the 2006 State survey to improve its forest area estimation procedures. The purpose of the Pee Dee special study was to independently estimate forest area on an intensive network of plots within the five-county area and compare the results to the FIA estimate of forest land.

## Methods

SCFC-FIA foresters used 2006 digital imagery to classify land use on a total of 1,455 plots in the five Pee Dee counties—three times the normal intensity of FIA sampled plots. Each plot was classified as forest, nonforest, or water according to FIA protocols for land use. Followup field evaluations were made for 421 plots where land use could not be classified conclusively from photography, including 90 plots where land use classification differed from a 2005 photointerpretation. The remaining 331 plots were visited because they fell along paved roads or near urban development,

were located along stand edges, had early-succession vegetation, or were obscured by shadow or cloud cover.

Once all ground visits were completed, the land use data for all 1,455 plots were used to estimate forest area and sampling errors using methods provided by Steel and others (1997). For comparison, similar calculations were made using current FIA procedures (Bechtold and Patterson 2005) and National Land Cover Data for stratification.

## Results

The forest area estimate from the Pee Dee special study was not statistically different from the FIA estimate for the five counties. In fact, there were no significant differences in the forest area estimates compared to photo-based single-, double-or triple-intensity sampling. While results from this study do not explain the reason for the apparent increase in forest area, the results do support the FIA area estimate derived from the current stratified estimation procedures.

As South Carolina Forestry Commission crews crisscrossed the Pee Dee area visiting plot locations, they also noted the lack of widespread change in land use from past aerial photographs. Limited forested areas, such as the Waccamaw Neck section of Georgetown County, SC, are being actively developed and early signs of more developments are appearing further inland. So far, development has not been widespread enough over the entire region to cause significant loss of forest land. However, this does indicate the need for monitoring and assessment of forests on the fringe of urban centers where land use change has a higher probability of occurring.

## Change in Timberland Area: Comparisons Over Time

The primary component of forest land is timberland, defined as land capable of growing at least 20 cubic feet of industrial wood per acre per year. The focus for the remainder of the report will be discussion of the timberland component of South Carolina's forest resource.

Timberland area in South Carolina has averaged around 12.4 million acres since the 1968 survey (fig. 2). Oscillations in timberland area estimates have occurred with some regularity in the past, including an increase of nearly 500,000 acres between 1958 and 1968, and a decline of 324,000 acres between 1978 and 1986. The low points in area over the past 40 years occurred in both 1986 and 2001 when timberland totaled an estimated 12.2 million acres. The peak estimate for timberland area occurred during the 2006 survey at 12.8 million acres, an increase of 579,000 acres over published 2001 FIA estimates.

These "snapshots" of timberland area estimates reflect sampled or "real" changes over time and, in some cases, include change introduced by alterations in data collection or data processing procedures. The increase in timberland area since 2001 is the largest ever observed between successive FIA surveys. However, the implementation of improved sampling methods for the 2006 survey resulted in basic differences in how the 2001 and 2006 inventories were conducted (see Appendix A—Inventory Methods). When survey

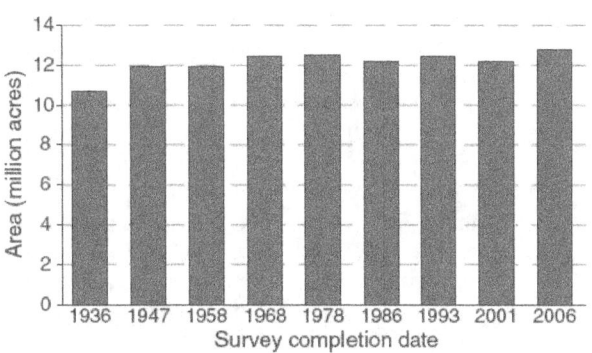

Figure 2—Area of timberland in South Carolina, 1936 to 2006.

methods are consistent between surveys, and sampling error is estimated to be within acceptable limits, direct comparisons can be made and changes in resource estimates explained largely in terms of sampled differences. When methods are altered between surveys, it can be difficult, if not impossible, to separate sampled change from change influenced by differences in survey methods.

Undoubtedly, a portion of the increase in timberland area since 2001 is the result of encountering real changes in land use occurring over the past 5 years—natural reversions or planting on nonforest land, for example. Accounting for sampled change can be accomplished by analyzing estimates of timberland additions and diversions based on the land use changes found at remeasured inventory locations (plots). These remeasured plots are data collection points sampled in both the 2001 and 2006 inventories.

Accounting for differences in resource estimates due to changes in survey methods is more difficult. Conducting the survey simultaneously using both the previous and current methods would do the task best, but would be impractical. An alternative would be to make the results from the two inventories as comparable as possible. One means of accomplishing this is to use the current sampling and processing procedures to reprocess the 2001 data (collected on plots common to both the 2001 and 2006 inventories). Comparing the revised 2001 estimate of timberland area to the 2006 estimate would account for some of the influences introduced by changes in inventory methods.

### Revised 2001 Estimate of Timberland Area

The published timberland estimate for 2001 was 12.22 million acres (Conner and others 2004). Using current inventory methods and processing procedures applied to the remeasured plots from the 2001 survey, the revised estimate for timberland area would amount to about 12.41 million acres. Applying the current forest resource inventory methods to the previous survey introduces the possibility that timberland area may have been underestimated by nearly 200,000 acres in 2001. If so, the revised increase in timberland area since 2001 would have been 388,000 acres (compared to the 579,000-acre difference between the 2001 reported estimate and the 2006 estimate). The revised increase would be well within the range of changes in timberland area reported by earlier surveys.

It should be noted that the 2001 forest resource estimates for South Carolina will remain as published. Revising the 2001 estimate of timberland area was done here only to illustrate how changes in inventory procedures might impact reported differences in timberland area.

### Accounting for Change in Timberland Area: Revised Additions and Diversions

FIA estimates of changes in land use between surveys, based on remeasured plots, are used to help explain changes in timberland area. Land use changes that add to the timberland base are collectively referred to as additions. Changes in land use that reduce timberland area are diversions. Additions typically result from previously nonforest land that has reverted naturally or was planted to a forested condition. Diversions occur when forest land is converted to some nonforest use, most often due to urban and other development, or clearing for agricultural use.

Table 6 provides a summary of the timberland additions and diversions—based on remeasured plots—occurring during the 2001 and 2006 surveys. To arrive at the revised 2001 survey estimate of timberland area (12.41 million acres), diversions to urban and other development would have removed almost 368,000 acres of previously forested land, while diversions to agricultural uses would have reduced the timber base by another 134,000 acres. Comparing these revised estimates to the previously reported 500,000 acres of timberland diverted to urban and

other development and the 182,000 acres removed for agriculture (see fig. 2 in Conner and others 2004), the 2001 survey may have overestimated the loss of timberland to urban and agricultural uses by a combined 180,000 acres. Timberland additions of nearly 494,000 acres—mostly from nonforest—would offset some of the timberland diverted to a nonforest use. The result is a revised net loss of <43,000 acres, rather than the reported decline of 230,000 acres using the published 2001 estimate.

Changes to timberland area resulted in a net gain of >388,000 acres, from the revised 2001 estimate of 12.41 million acres to 12.8 million acres in 2006 (table 6). Estimates of diversions to urban and agriculture, though considerably lower than the previous survey, reduced the timber base by a combined 253,000 acres. However, the reduction was more than offset by substantial additions to timberland area, resulting in the 388,000-acre net increase. Figure 3 summarizes the acres of additions and diversions to timberland for the 2001 and 2006 surveys, using the revised 2001 timberland area estimate.

Procedural differences make it difficult to separate differences in resource estimates due to sampled change from differences introduced by inconsistencies in survey methods. When methods are altered between surveys, it is prudent to use caution when trying to compare results or establish trends in area or any other resource estimate. The preceding analysis was provided to illustrate one approach to approximating the impacts that changes in inventory methods can have on forest resource estimates—in this case, differences in estimates of timberland area.

**Table 6—Land-use change in South Carolina for the previous (1993 to 2001) and current (2001 to 2006) survey periods**

| Land-use change | 1993 | 2001 |
|---|---|---|
| | *acres* | |
| Area of timberland | 12,454,925 | 12,412,400 |
| Additions to timberland from | | |
|   Nonforest | 460,401 | 694,973 |
|   Noncommercial | 33,142 | 0 |
|   Nonsampled | 0 | 36,577 |
|     Total additions | 493,543 | 731,550 |
| Diversions from timberland to | | |
|   Other forest land | 5,126 | 17,612 |
|   Nonsampled | 0 | 16,870 |
|   Agriculture | 134,169 | 104,765 |
|   Urban and other nonforest | 367,730 | 148,190 |
|   Water | 29,043 | 55,871 |
|     Total diversions | 536,068 | 343,308 |
| Net change[a] | -42,525 | 388,242 |
| | 2001[b] | 2006 |
| Area of timberland | 12,412,400 | 12,800,642 |

[a] Net change = additions - diversions.
[b] Data from the 2001 Forest Inventory and Analysis survey were reprocessed using current data collection and processing procedures. Doing so makes the data from both surveys more compatible and makes direct comparisons possible.

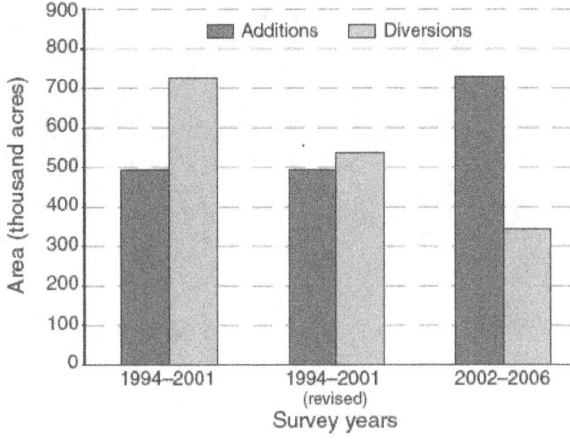

Figure 3—Timberland area additions and diversions for selected survey periods, South Carolina.

# Forest Composition and Stand Structure

Some 120 tree species were encountered during the 2006 inventory of South Carolina (appendix C). The most common naturally occurring softwood species in the State, and throughout the South, is loblolly pine. Loblolly pine is also the tree species of choice for planting, which adds to its widespread occurrence. Red and white oak species, commonly found in most Southeast States, are South Carolina's dominant hardwoods. These common species mix with other softwoods and hardwoods to form defined forest types. These forest types and the sizes of trees present make up the composition and structure of the forests in South Carolina. Identifying stand origin—indicating whether a stand was established naturally or through planting—further adds to the description of the State's forest resources.

## Forest Management Types: Combining Forest Type and Stand Origin

Forest types—named for the species forming a plurality of stand stocking—can be aggregated into three broad groups: softwoods, hardwoods, and oak-pine hardwood stands. The forest types making up the hardwood group can be subdivided into upland and lowland types based on the specific species present. The oak-pine forest-type group is composed of a predominance of hardwood trees with a pine component accounting for at least 25 percent of stand stocking. These mixed oak-pine stands often occur naturally, but can also result from hardwood species regenerating in a planted pine stand. Stand origin differentiates natural from planted stands and is determined for all forested acres. FIA combines forest type and stand origin information to form forest management types.

The distribution of forest management types over the past 30 years is shown in figure 4. Two general points can be taken from the chart. The first is the change in area of pine from a predominance of natural stands to a plurality of planted pine. The second point is the relatively moderate fluctuations in area of upland and lowland hardwood types and oak-pine.

Historically, pine forests have accounted for roughly one-half of the total forest area of South Carolina; and early on, natural stands were the rule. In 1978, FIA reported 4.2 million acres of natural pine (Knight and McClure 1979), more than three times the area of planted pine. Over the ensuing years, government tree planting incentives and increased harvesting followed by

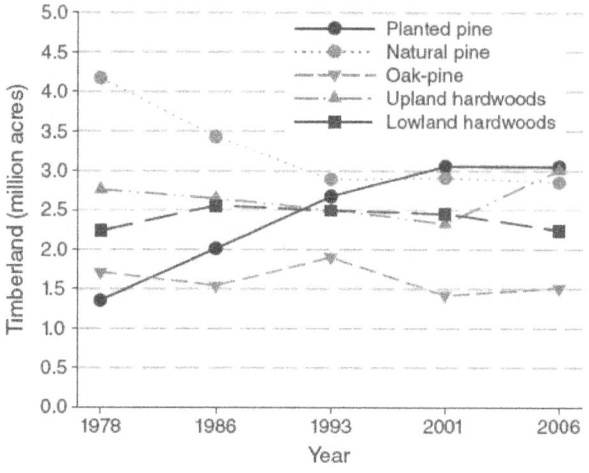

Figure 4—Area of timberland by forest-management type in South Carolina.

artificial regeneration resulted in the shift from natural pine stands to increasingly more planted pine acres. By 2001, planted pine acres outnumbered natural stands. As of 2006, planted pine accounts for nearly 3.1 million acres, exceeding natural pine stands by about 207,000 acres. However, the rate at which planted pine was replacing natural stands declined between the 1993 and 2001 FIA surveys.

The reduced rate of increase in planted stands can be partly traced to the divestiture of forest land by forest industry. Planting, harvesting, and replanting was a cycle often repeated on forest industry timberland. Many of the formerly forest industry-owned acres are now held by new owners with widely differing desires to manage or capabilities to invest in their forest land. Figure 5 provides estimates of acres planted since 1987. The peak in acres planted for this time period occurred in 1988 when 233,000 acres were artificially regenerated, including 71,000 acres on forest industry timberland. The majority of the planting occurred on privately owned timberlands in response to timber markets and to federal cost-share incentives such as the

Cypress at Woods Bay State Natural Area, a large Carolina Bay in coastal South Carolina.

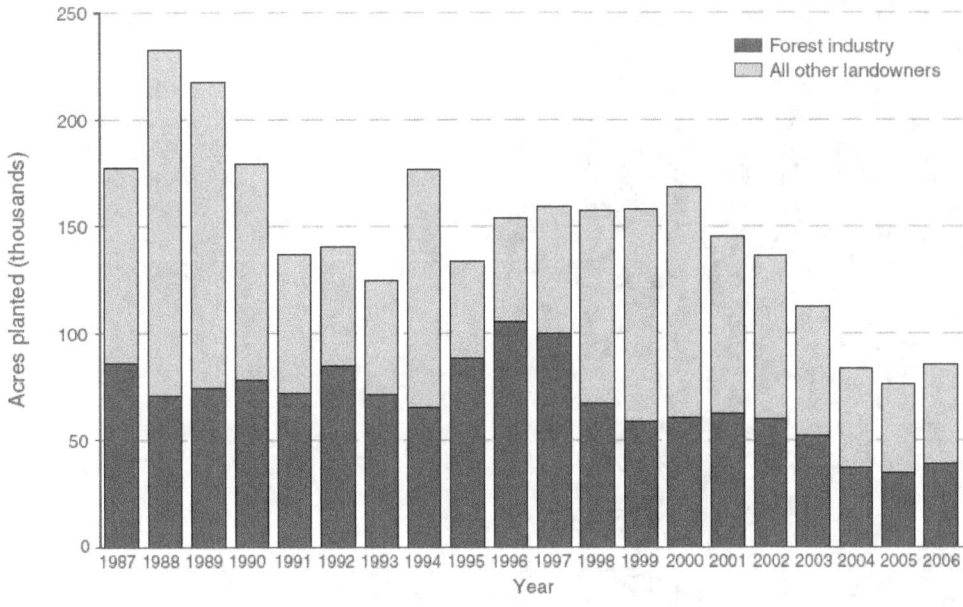

Figure 5—Acres of timberland planted by year, South Carolina, 1987 to 2006.

Conservation Reserve Program. From the peak year, tree planting in South Carolina has trended downward. The decline in planting over the past 6 years has been precipitous, falling from 168,000 acres in 2000 to little more than one-half that number (85,000 acres) in 2006. Forest industry's contribution to the latest estimate is just 39,000 acres.

A reduction in acres undergoing a final harvest has had a strong influence on the recent downward trend in tree planting. Between 1987 and 1993, FIA estimates

showed more than 279,000 acres were final harvested annually, totaling nearly 1.7 million acres over the 6-year period. This peak in harvesting was accompanied by a peak in annual planting as nearly 152,000 acres (911,000 acres over 6 years) were artificially regenerated:

| Survey period | Annual final harvest | Regenerated annually | | |
|---|---|---|---|---|
| | | Natural | Artificial | Total |
| | | acres | | |
| 1979–1986 | 257,858 | 150,991 | 111,897 | 262,888 |
| 1987–1993 | 279,037 | 219,844 | 151,796 | 371,640 |
| 1994–2001 | 189,300 | 133,900 | 124,900 | 258,800 |
| 2002–2006 | 167,880 | 49,800 | 94,650 | 144,450 |

As the acres undergoing a final harvest declined, so did acres being artificially regenerated. By the 2002 to 2006 survey period, final harvest acres dropped below 168,000 per year and planting averaged <95,000 acres annually. Moreover, the 2002 to 2006 survey period marked the first time in more than 2 decades that acres regenerated from natural and artificial means combined fell below final harvest acres.

Whatever the reasons, the result is fewer acres are being planted, and the current downturn in local timber markets will likely add to the reduction. Nonetheless, planted pine continues to play an important role in South Carolina's timber industry, accounting for a large portion of the State's timberland area, softwood volume, growth, and removals (see sidebar, next page).

A natural hardwood stand along a small coastal creek in Sumter County.

16

# The Contribution of Planted Pine to South Carolina's Timberland Resources

The area of planted pine in South Carolina has been on the rise since FIA began to recognize stand origin as a separate classification. Recent factors such as forest industry's divestiture of its landholdings, reduced planting incentives, and an economic downturn have all contributed to the reduction in the rate of tree planting in the State. As a result, rather than the typical increase in planted pine area witnessed by previous surveys, the number of planted pine acres remained relatively unchanged since 2001. However, at almost 3.1 million acres planted pine stands still comprise nearly one-quarter of the total area of timberland, and outnumber natural pine stands by 207,000 acres. Planted stands account for 4.4 billion cubic feet (21 percent) of all live volume, 493 million cubic feet (41 percent) of net annual growth, and 314 million cubic feet (39 percent) of annual removals:

| Forest management type | Timberland (excludes nonstocked) | All-live volume | Net annual growth | Annual removals |
|---|---|---|---|---|
| | *million acres* | ------ *million cubic feet* ------ | | |
| Planted pine | 3.1 | 4,429.6 | 493.4 | 314.0 |
| Natural pine | 2.8 | 5,202.0 | 261.9 | 238.0 |
| Hardwoods | 6.8 | 11,847.3 | 448.2 | 262.2 |
| Total | 12.7 | 21,478.9 | 1,203.5 | 814.2 |

With so much of the pine resource in planted stands, continuing to plant on nonforest land and regenerate timberland acres after harvest are crucial factors to sustaining the productive capacity of South Carolina's pine timberland.

Managed longleaf pine stand on Manchester State Forest in Sumter County.

The second point to note from figure 4 is that, although some modulation in the area of hardwoods has occurred over time, there has been a general consistency in acres of hardwood and oak-pine types. The area of oak-pine has hovered between 1.4 and 1.9 million acres since 1978, and is currently at 1.5 million acres. Area in lowland hardwood types was reported to be 2.2 million acres in 1978, peaked at just <2.6 million acres in 1986, but by 2006 has declined to the 1978 level of 2.2 million acres. One notable change, however, is the rather significant increase in upland hardwoods since 2001. From the nearly 2.8 million acres reported in 1978, the area of upland hardwoods declined to a low point of 2.3 million acres in 2001. Just 5 years later there are >3.0 million acres of upland hardwood forest types scattered across the State.

Movement of stands among forest-type groups occurs with some regularity as natural disturbance, harvesting, or normal stand development changes tree species stocking enough to warrant reclassification. The increase in upland hardwoods is a case in point. The majority (45 percent) of the increase in upland hardwood area came from what were previously oak-pine stands where the pine component is now no longer present in necessary levels to maintain the oak-pine classification. Recent outbreaks of southern pine beetle (*Dendroctonus frontalis*) likely played a role in reducing or even eliminating pine stocking in what were oak-pine stands. Another one-quarter (26 percent) of the increase came from formerly pine acres where natural regeneration to an upland type followed a final harvest.

About 8 percent of the additional acres of upland hardwood timberland were the result of natural regeneration (reversion) on nonforest land.

## Stand-Size Distributions

Stand-size classifications are based on the diameter-class distribution of live trees in the stand. Classifying stands as sawtimber, poletimber, or sapling-seedling helps define the structure of each stand. Typically, stands are stocked by trees of varying diameters. However, sawtimber stands have a predominance of large-diameter trees (≥9.0 inches diameter at breast height (d.b.h.) for softwoods, ≥ 11.0 inches d.b.h. for hardwoods) making up stand stocking. The average tree diameter in poletimber stands ranges from a minimum of 5.0 inches up to sawtimber size. Sapling-seedling stands have a predominance of trees <5.0 inches d.b.h.

Compared to softwoods, the lower demand for hardwood products and generally higher resistance to damage or mortality from weather events often results in more hardwood stands reaching sawtimber size. The majority (3.4 million) of the nearly 6.0 million acres of sawtimber in South Carolina in 2006 (fig. 6) are hardwoods. However, it appears that more of South Carolina's softwood stands are being managed for sawtimber. As of 2006, softwood sawtimber amounted to 2.5 million acres or 43 percent of the current area of forest land in this size class. Softwood sawtimber amounted to 1.9 million acres in 2001.

Overall, the 6.0 million acres of sawtimber in 2006 is 1.6 million acres more than were present in 2001. This increase is the result of smaller diameter stands growing into the sawtimber class and sawtimber stands on timberland acres included in the survey for the first time. The 2006 estimate of sawtimber is one-half million acres more than were reported in 1986, 3 years before Hurricane Hugo struck and reduced sawtimber stands by nearly 750,000 acres.

Area of poletimber declined by nearly 700,000 acres since 2001 to 3.5 million (fig. 6), but the decline includes the acres moving into sawtimber. At nearly 2.0 million acres, softwood poletimber stands outnumber hardwood poletimber by nearly 500,000 in 2006. Sapling-seedling stands have declined by 350,000 acres over the past 5 years, and now occupy nearly 3.3 million acres. Hardwoods account for almost 58 percent of the sapling-seedling stands.

## Stand Age

The age of a forest stand is based on the average age of the trees in the predominant size class at the time of the inventory. Figure 7 displays the distribution of stocked hardwood timberland acres by stand age for the 2001 and 2006 surveys. Current estimates show that hardwood acreage has increased in nearly all the younger age classes up through stands 51 to 55 years old. One-third of South Carolina's 6.8 million acres of hardwood stands average

≤ 20 years in age. Hardwood stands older than 75 years amounted to 638,000 acres, down from 705,000 acres in 2001. Younger stands are generally more vigorous, therefore the increased acreage of young hardwood stands could result in higher hardwood productivity and lower mortality in the future.

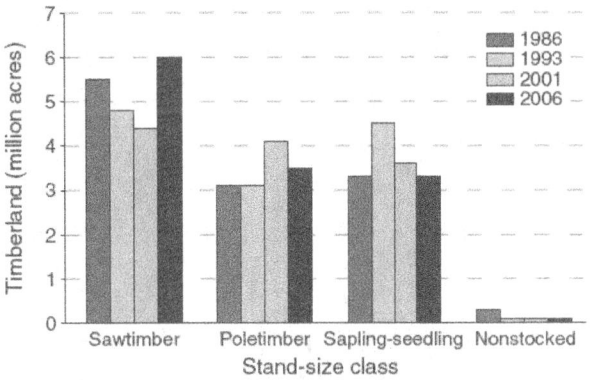

Figure 6— Area of timberland by stand-size class and survey year, South Carolina.

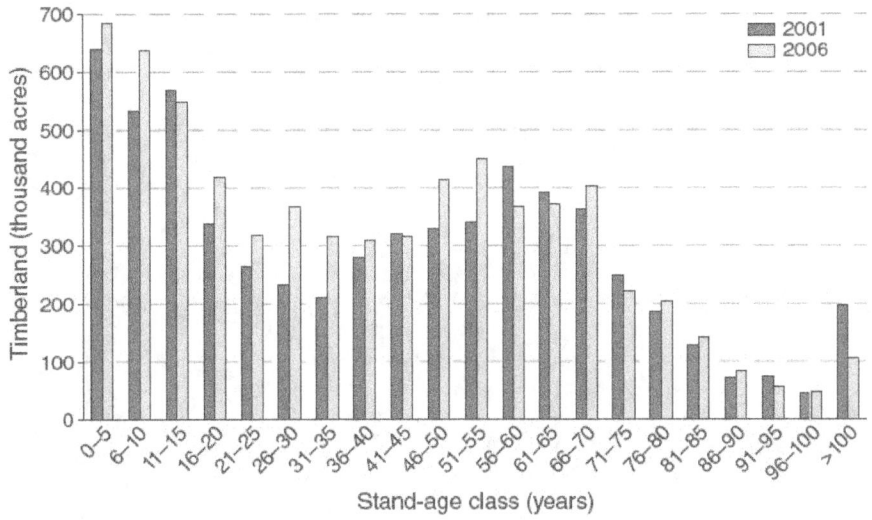

Figure 7—Distribution of hardwood timberland by stand-age class, South Carolina, 2001 and 2006.

Softwood timberland acreage in stands ≤15 years of age declined by >675,000 acres since 2001 (fig. 8), further indication of the reduction in tree planting efforts. Combined acreage in older age classes (>35 years) also declined since 2001, falling from 1.5 million acres to 1.3 million. Conversely, combined area in stands ranging from 16 to 35 years old increased from 1.9 million acres in 2001 to 2.7 million in 2006. These classes make up the majority of the softwood stands of harvestable age—particularly true of planted stands—and they hold a

large portion of South Carolina's current surplus of wood volume. Many members of the forest products industry anticipate that this volume will soon be arriving at the State's numerous forest products mills. The ample supply of wood bodes well for the near term; however, the recent decline in tree planting (fig. 5) raises concerns about regeneration of these stands once they are harvested. Continued reductions in tree planting will make it more difficult over the long term to maintain the State's pine resource at current levels.

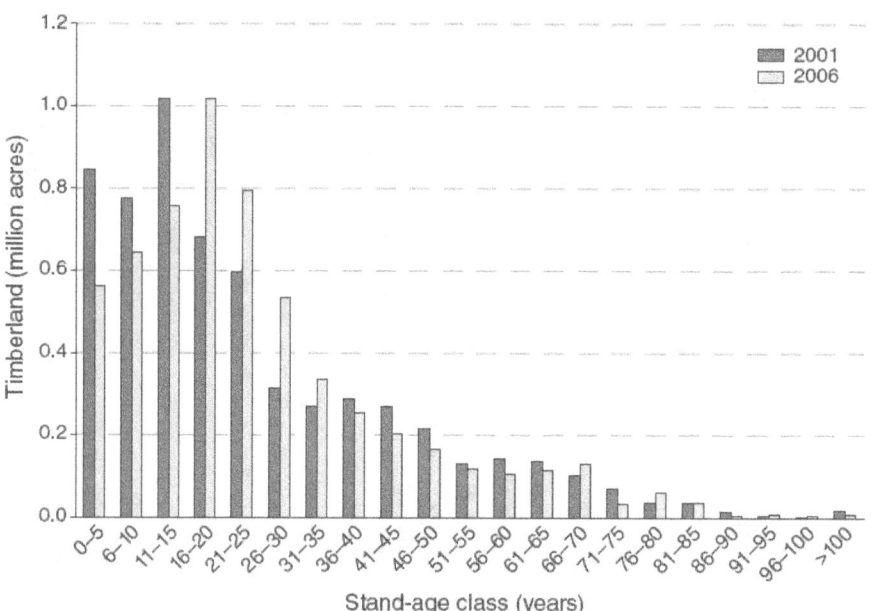

Figure 8—Distribution of softwood timberland by stand-age class, South Carolina, 2001 and 2006.

# Live Tree Volume and South Carolina's "Wall of Wood"

As of 2006, total all live volume on timberland in South Carolina amounted to 21.5 billion cubic feet, the most volume ever reported for the State. All live volume has increased about 1.8 billion cubic feet since 2001, and is up 3.6 billion over 1993 estimates which reflected losses from Hurricane Hugo's 1989 trek across the southeastern portion of the State.

Current all live volume is split almost evenly between softwoods (10.6 billion cubic feet) and hardwoods (10.9 billion cubic feet). The red and white oak species groups combined accounted for nearly 4.0 billion cubic feet (37 percent) of the current hardwood volume. The loblolly and shortleaf pine species group accounted for 8.8 billion cubic feet (83 percent) of the softwood volume. This included 4.4 billion cubic feet of live softwood volume in planted pine stands, South Carolina's contribution to the "wall of wood" that has accumulated in pine plantations throughout the South. These pine stands, many planted as a result of government incentives in the mid-1980s, have steadily increased in volume as they grew from pulpwood to sawtimber size.

The increased volume in 2006 is to be expected in light of the 600,000-acre increase in timberland area since 2001. "New" acres of timberland usually bring with them additional volume; how much depends on their current condition and stage of development when they are incorporated into the FIA survey. Recently forested acres—natural reversions or planted acres—on average contain very little volume. On older, well-stocked forested acres, the additional volume can be substantial. Per acre estimates of all live volume over time reflect this changing mix of young and old stands added to the inventory, and also reflect the volume growth on remeasured forested acres.

All live volume averaged almost 1,679 cubic feet per acre in 2006, outpacing the average volume per acre for the three previous surveys:

| Survey year | All live volume per acre | | |
| --- | --- | --- | --- |
| | Softwoods | Hardwoods | Total |
| | cubic feet | | |
| 1986 | 1,642.4 | 1,523.0 | 1,576.3 |
| 1993 | 1,455.4 | 1,418.2 | 1,434.8 |
| 2001 | 1,567.4 | 1,653.1 | 1,611.3 |
| 2006 | 1,801.1 | 1,574.0 | 1,678.7 |

The increased volume per acre for all timberland is bolstered by 1,801 cubic feet of volume per acre for softwoods. The previous discussion of the age-class distribution for softwood timberland pointed out the large proportion of acres in stands 16 to 35 years old, the prime harvestable age classes in terms of volume. The current high softwood volume per acre and the abundance of older, large-diameter pine stands underscores the potential for industry growth to take advantage of the increased volume in pine pulpwood and small saw logs.

The distribution of all live volume by diameter class reinforces the general differences between the age and structure of hardwood and softwood stands. Hardwood stands, generally stocked with older and larger trees, contain 43 percent of the current hardwood volume in trees ≥16 inches d.b.h. In fact, there has never been more volume in any of these larger diameter classes than that reported in 2006. Hardwood volume has increased by 520 million cubic feet since 2001, and 396 million cubic feet (76 percent) of that increase was in trees with diameters ≥16 inches (fig. 9). As is often the case, South Carolina has a wealth of underutilized hardwood volume in large saw-log trees.

Softwood volume increased by nearly 1.3 billion cubic feet since 2001, and 840 million cubic feet (66 percent) of the increase occurred in diameter classes ≤12 inches (fig. 10). In contrast to hardwoods, only 27 percent of the softwood all live volume is in trees ≥16 inches d.b.h. However, softwood volume did increase in all diameter classes. Moreover, the softwood volume reported in most diameter classes in 2006 exceeds any previous estimate. It is uncertain whether this signals the beginning of a shift in management strategy away from pulpwood and toward sawtimber as the primary forest product.

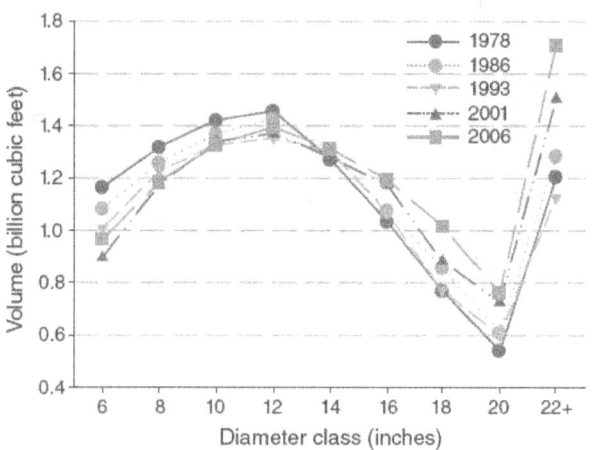

Figure 9—All live hardwood volume on timberland by diameter class and survey year, South Carolina.

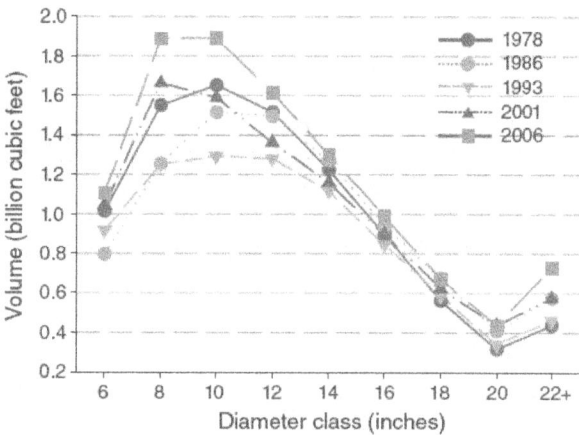

Figure 10—All live softwood volume on timberland by diameter class and survey year, South Carolina.

South Carolina Forestry Commission forester works with logger to minimize impacts from harvest.

## Timberland Net Annual Growth and Removals

Timberland net annual growth and removals estimates are average annual values for the survey period. For the 2006 survey, the net growth and removals estimates represent the average annual values for years 2002 to 2006. Total net annual growth of all live trees on timberland continued to increase at an incredible rate. Over the recent 5-year survey period, net growth averaged > 1.2 billion cubic feet per year for a total of about 6.0 billion cubic feet of wood added to the inventory. The current growth rate surpasses by far any previous rate of volume growth seen in South Carolina.

Between 2002 and 2006, net growth for all live softwood trees on timberland averaged 817.0 million cubic feet per year, outpacing what was the high mark for softwood growth of 691.8 million cubic feet per year set during the previous survey period (fig. 11). Removals averaged 596.1 million cubic feet per year during the 2006 survey, for a growth-to-cut ratio of 1.37 to 1.0. This means that at the State level, South Carolina forests are producing about 37 percent more softwood volume than is currently being harvested.

The State's hardwood timberland resource is also in good shape with respect to its growth-to-cut ratio. Statewide, hardwoods are growing wood at a rate of 387.3 million cubic feet per year, an increase of 27 percent over the record-setting mark of 305.9 million cubic feet per year set during the previous survey. Hardwood annual removals dropped from an average of 250.7 million cubic feet per year between 1994 and 2001, to 217.7 million cubic feet per year for the current survey (fig. 12). Hardwood growth-to-cut ratio statewide improved from 1.2 to 1.0 during the previous survey, to the current 1.8 to 1.0 ratio.

Comparing the rate of growth per acre for current and previous surveys provides a better perspective on the average amount of wood that is being added annually to each timberland acre:

| Survey period | All live net annual growth per acre | | |
| | Softwoods | Hardwoods | Total |
| --- | --- | --- | --- |
| | *cubic feet* | | |
| 1979–1986 | 82.6 | 38.5 | 58.2 |
| 1987–1993 | 62.2 | 27.2 | 42.9 |
| 1994–2001 | 116.0 | 48.9 | 81.6 |
| 2002–2006 | 138.5 | 56.1 | 94.1 |

At the 2002 to 2006 rate of growth, an average of 94.1 cubic feet of wood are being added annually to timberland acres in South Carolina. Currently, an average softwood stand is growing wood at 138.5 cubic feet per acre per year. That is equivalent to adding the volume of fifty-eight, 6-inch diameter pine trees to each acre of softwood timberland every year. Hardwood growth per acre averaged less than one-half that of softwoods, but the 2002 to 2006 rate of growth of 56.1 cubic feet per acre per year is the highest recorded for hardwood timberland.

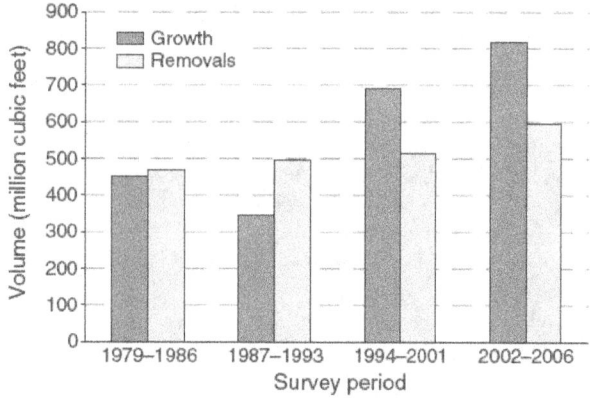

Figure 11—All live softwood net annual growth and removals on timberland by survey period, South Carolina.

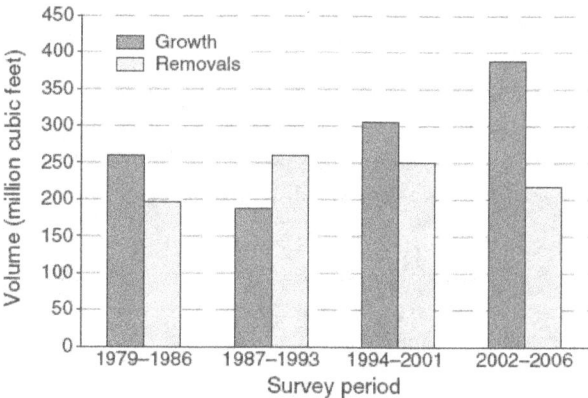

Figure 12— All live hardwood net annual growth and removals on timberland by survey period, South Carolina.

## South Carolina Forestry: A Growing Industry

South Carolina's forests have always played a critical role in the economic health of the State. With over 67 percent of the total land area in forests, this natural resource provides the raw materials to support a growing forest industry. Today, forestry is as important to South Carolina as it has ever been, contributing $17.45 billion to the State's economy and providing support for almost 45,000 families.

Forestry was one of the State's first industries in response to the need for housing, furniture, ship-building materials, and fuelwood. Kingstree, one of South Carolina's earliest settlements, was named for the colonial use of its pine forests by the King of England. South Carolina's forest industry has evolved from its early sawmilling and naval stores history to a diverse industry that produces everything from traditional products to clonal seedlings and state-of-the-art wood energy plants. Favorable markets and an abundant wood supply have attracted new forest industry to South Carolina. Existing industry has also expanded to take advantage of increasing consumer demand.

The magnitude of the forest industry has grown steadily throughout South Carolina's history. Production of primary timber products has more than tripled within the past 70 years, growing from 188.7 million cubic feet in 1936 to 645.2 million cubic feet in 2005 (Johnson and Smith 2007). Although industrial growth has been interrupted periodically by periods of recession (the most recent downturn occurred after the turn of the century), once the additional production capacity from newly announced industrial expansions are added (fig. 13), South

The Grant Forest Products mill began producing oriented-strand board in the fall of 2006. (photo courtesy of the South Carolina Forestry Commission)

Forest-based recreation contributes $483 million to the State's economy.

Carolina forest industry will be producing more forest products than ever recorded in its history.

Forestry is now a $17.45 billion dollar industry in South Carolina. This is a conservative estimate in that by 2006 the new mill expansions were only in their startup phases. While many manufacturing jobs in other industries have gone overseas, Impact Analysis for Planning (IMPLAN) analysis clearly shows that forest industry's impact on the State's economy has grown (South Carolina Forestry Commission 2008).

An IMPLAN analysis, based on 2006 economic data, was completed by the South Carolina Forestry Commission with

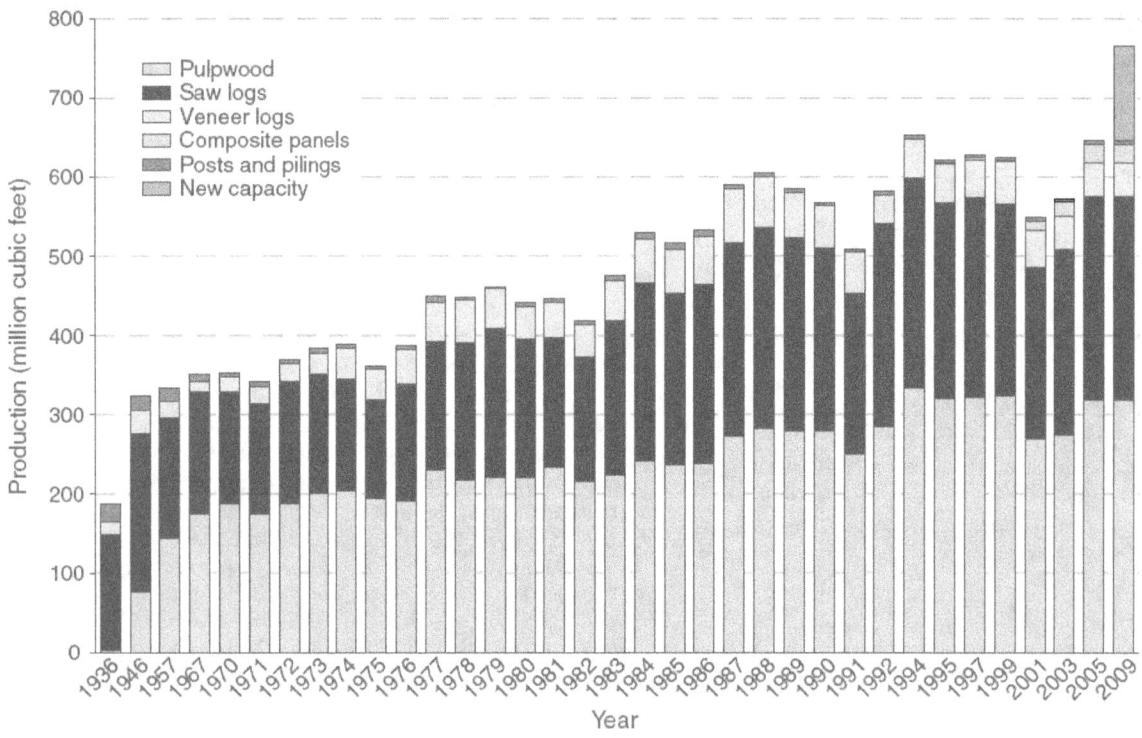

Figure 13—Production of primary timber products in South Carolina, 1936 to 2005. The 2009 estimate adds the new mill capacity to the 2005 production levels.

assistance from Clemson University. The overall goal of the study was to characterize the economic impact of all major aspects of forestry to South Carolina's economy. This study is unique from past studies in that a special effort was made to identify and quantify the contributions made by forestry-based businesses that are traditionally classified within other economic sectors. Examples of these "additions" include the pine straw industry, certain wood-based chemical plants, shaving mills associated with the animal bedding industry, the bark and mulch industry, independent biomass plants, independent timber dealers, and public forestry employees.

Individual forestry-based business categories were grouped into six major forestry aggregate sectors: timber, logging, sawmills, wood furniture, pulp and paper, and forest-based recreation. Except for recreation and the other forestry-based additions, the aggregate sectors were based on the definitions and methodology used by Abt and others (2002). Direct, indirect, and induced effects were calculated for each aggregate sector. Aggregate sectors were described by four criteria: employment, labor income, value-added, and total industry output.

The pulp and paper industry is the dominant player in South Carolina's forest industry. In fact, pulp and paper contributes over one-half of forestry's total economic impact to the State's economy (table 7). The

State's seven pulp and paper plants are the major contributors to this aggregate sector, but chemical plants also make a significant contribution.

The sawmill aggregate sector includes a diverse mix of companies that all produce a solid wood product. Examples of these products include lumber, treated lumber, veneer, trusses, wood windows and doors, and pallets. This sector includes the bulk of South Carolina's 75 primary wood processors and approaches the

**Table 7—Economic effects of wood products sectors for South Carolina (based on Impact Analysis for Planning (IMPLAN) model results), 2006**

| Sector | Employment number | Labor income | Value added | Total industry output |
|---|---|---|---|---|
| | | ------- million dollars -------- | | |
| **Direct effects of aggregate wood products sectors** | | | | |
| Timber | 3,896 | 144 | 202 | 563 |
| Logging | 4,702 | 178 | 285 | 1,129 |
| Sawmills | 11,700 | 511 | 921 | 2,667 |
| Wood furniture | 4,435 | 189 | 299 | 672 |
| Pulp and paper | 13,803 | 1,247 | 2,063 | 6,298 |
| All wood products | 38,536 | 2,269 | 3,770 | 11,329 |
| Forest-based recreation | 6,172 | 162 | 270 | 483 |
| All forest products | 44,708 | 2,430 | 4,040 | 11,812 |
| **Total impact values[a]** | | | | |
| Timber | 8,572 | 300 | 414 | 917 |
| Logging | 10,344 | 346 | 556 | 1,736 |
| Sawmills | 20,106 | 871 | 1,584 | 3,973 |
| Wood furniture | 7,490 | 290 | 488 | 1,045 |
| Pulp and paper | 35,572 | 2,032 | 3,508 | 9,042 |
| All wood products | 82,084 | 3,839 | 6,550 | 16,713 |
| Forest-based recreation | 8,540 | 230 | 413 | 738 |
| All forest products | 90,624 | 4,069 | 6,963 | 17,451 |

Note: Methods were patterned after those in chapter 10 of the Southern Forest Resource Assessment (tables 10.2 and 10.3).

[a] Total impact values (direct+indirect+induced) for 2006 wood products output levels.

pulp and paper industry in total number of employees. The health of the sawmill and solid wood products sector is closely tied to the housing industry. In South Carolina, new housing starts reached an unprecedented high in 2005 before correcting somewhat in 2006.

The logging aggregate sector includes businesses that harvest, process, and transport timber from the forest to the mill. Direct employment within the logging sector totals 4,702 employees. The logging workforce is distributed throughout the State and it is often the most recognized aspect of forestry at the local level.

South Carolina's furniture industry employs 4,435 individuals with a labor income of $189 million. The single largest component of this industry sector is the construction of kitchen cabinets and countertops, employing 1,792 individuals. South Carolina's manufacturers can produce quality furniture that competes well globally.

Companies in the timber aggregate sector directly employ 3,896 individuals with a labor income of $144 million. The timber aggregate sector includes companies that own land for the purpose of selling timber, site preparation companies, forest tree seedling nurseries, tree planting contractors, and consultants. Federal, State, and university forestry employees were included in this sector as additions to traditional analyses.

Forest-based recreation, the smallest of the forestry aggregate sectors, contributes $483 million in direct impact to South Carolina's economy (fig. 14). The basic recreation data for selected hunting and other outdoor forest-based forms of recreation were taken from "2006 National Survey of Fishing, Hunting, and Wildlife-Associated Recreation" published by the U.S. Fish and Wildlife Service (U.S. Department of the Interior 2007).

In 1990, forestry ranked third for employment and fourth for labor income, respectively (Egbert and others 1992). In 2006, forestry has emerged as the leading manufacturing industry in South Carolina in terms of employment and labor income (fig. 15). Nearly 45,000 people, earning $2.43 billion in labor income, are directly employed in the forestry sector as defined

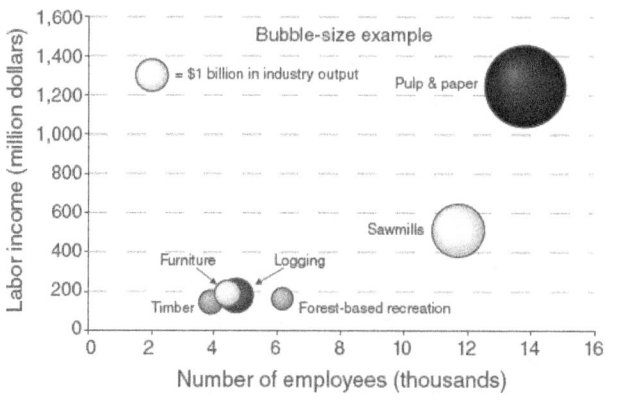

Figure 14—Direct economic effects of forestry sectors in South Carolina, 2006.

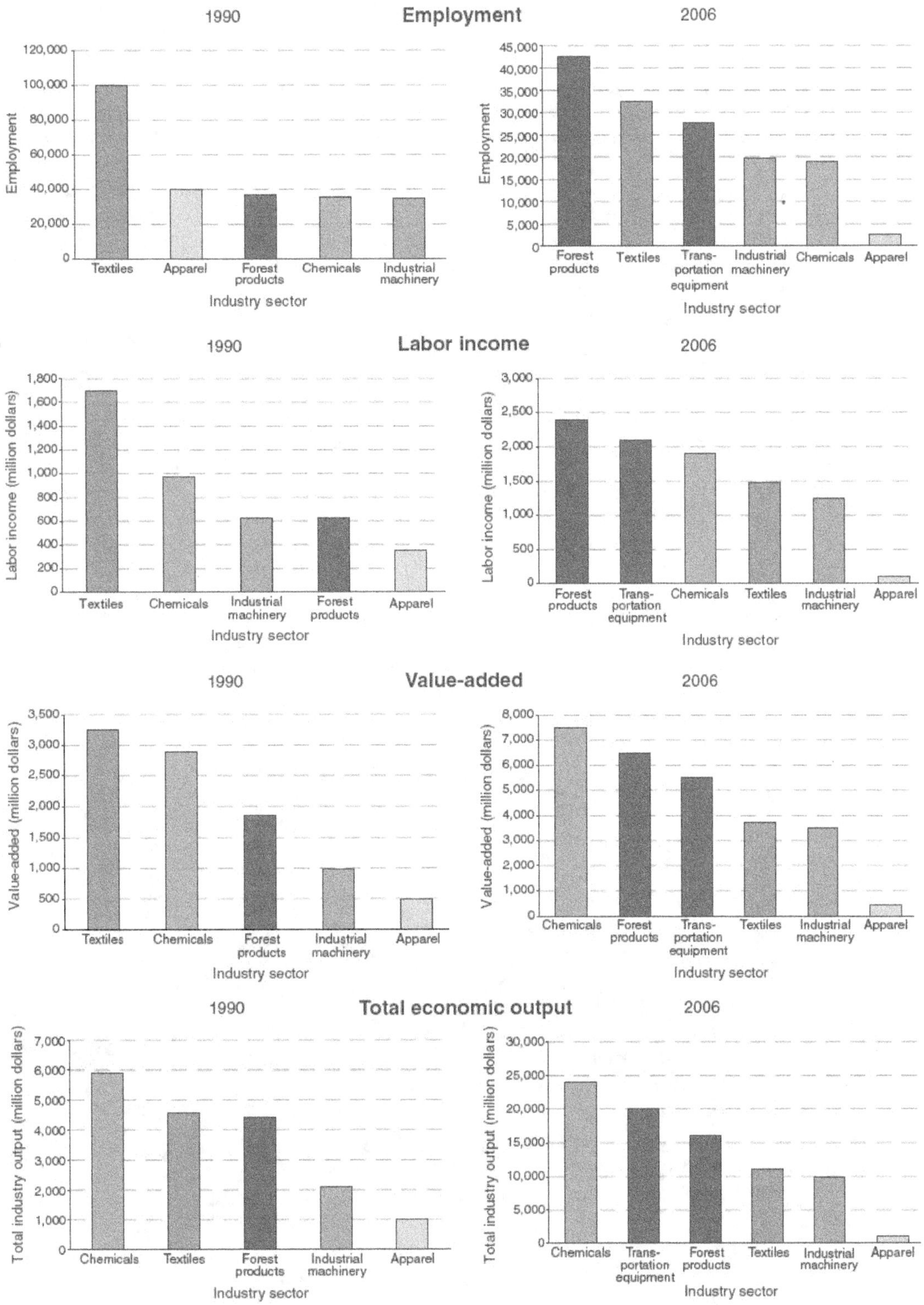

## Employment

**1990**

**2006**

## Labor income

**1990**

**2006**

## Value-added

**1990**

**2006**

## Total economic output

**1990**

**2006**

Figure 15—Ranking of major manufacturing industries in South Carolina, 1990 and 2006 (South Carolina Forestry Commission 2008).

by this study. A combination of growth in forest industry along with a dramatic decline in the textile industry over the past decade explains the prominence of forestry in the current study.

Forestry ranks second among manufacturing industries in terms of value-added and third in terms of total industry output. Industry output can be viewed as the value of shipment of the final products or total sales value. Value-added is the portion of the total industry output that can be attributed to production of the products in South Carolina. Forest products rank higher in value-added relative to other industries because many of the forest products are grown and manufactured locally.

## Timber Product Output

The diverse forest products industry in South Carolina is supplied by a variety of mills, ranging from small to medium-sized hardwood sawmills to the very large softwood sawmills, pulpmills, and plywood mills. In 2005, there were about 75 sawmills, pulpwood mills, and other primary wood-processing plants distributed across the State (fig. 16). This section presents estimates of average annual roundwood product output and timber removals for the period 2001 through 2005.

Estimates of timber product output (TPO) and plant residues were obtained from canvasses (questionnaires) sent to all major primary wood-using mills in the State. The canvasses are used to determine the types and amount of roundwood (i.e., saw logs, pulpwood, plywood and veneer, poles, etc.) received by each mill, the county of origin of the wood, the species used, and how mills disposed of the bark and wood residues produced. The canvasses were conducted every 2 years by personnel from the Southern Research Station and South Carolina Forestry Commission. These data are used to augment FIA's

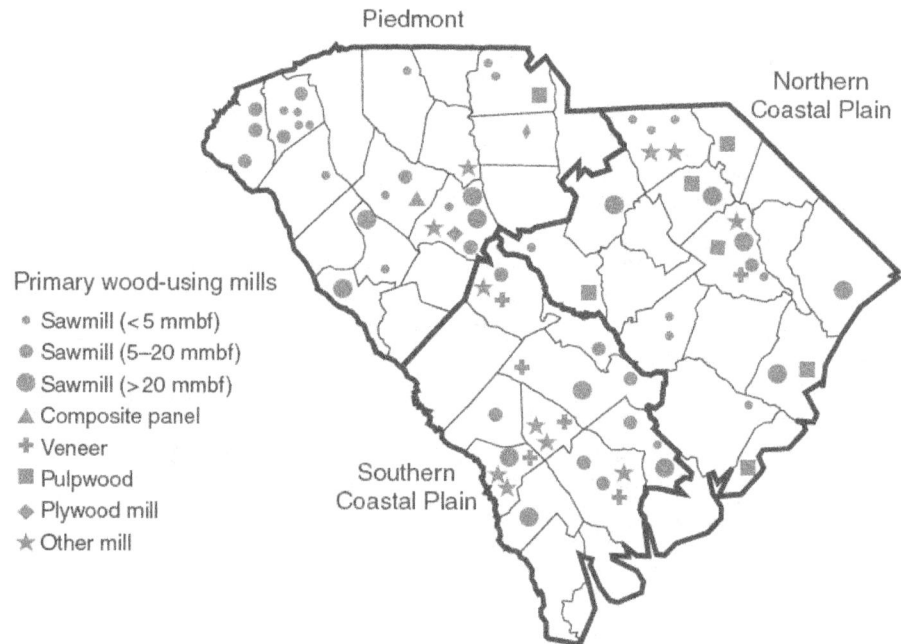

Figure 16—Primary wood-using mills in South Carolina, 2005.

annual inventory of timber removals by providing the product proportions for that segment of removals that is used for products. Individual studies are necessary to track trends and changes in product output levels.

Industry surveys conducted in 2001, 2003, and 2005 were used to determine average annual product output for roundwood and plant byproducts for the latest survey period (Johnson and Knight 2006, Johnson and Smith 2007, Johnson and others 2004). Therefore, volumes reported for individual products are an average value per year and will not match specific year values or reports where all years are reported. Total product output, averaged over the survey period, is the sum of the volume of roundwood products from all sources (growing stock and other sources) and the volume of plant byproducts, or mill residues.

Total output of timber products, which includes domestic fuelwood and plant byproducts, averaged 755 million cubic feet per year between 2001 and 2005 (table 8). Eighty-nine percent, or 669 million cubic feet, of the total output was from roundwood products, while the remainder was from plant byproducts (mill residue). Softwood species provided 81 percent (615 million cubic feet) of the total product output volume. Hardwoods provided the remaining 19 percent (140 million cubic feet) of total output.

Table 8—Average annual output of timber products by product, species group, and type of material, South Carolina, 2001 to 2005

| Product and species group | Total output | Roundwood products | Plant byproducts |
|---|---|---|---|
| | | *million cubic feet* | |
| **Saw logs** | | | |
| Softwood | 235.6 | 234.0 | 1.6 |
| Hardwood | 25.6 | 25.6 | 0.0 |
| Total | 261.2 | 259.6 | 1.6 |
| **Veneer logs** | | | |
| Softwood | 34.3 | 34.3 | — |
| Hardwood | 7.1 | 7.1 | — |
| Total | 41.4 | 41.4 | — |
| **Pulpwood**[a] | | | |
| Softwood | 289.6 | 236.5 | 53.1 |
| Hardwood | 79.5 | 74.8 | 4.8 |
| Total | 369.1 | 311.3 | 57.9 |
| **Composite panels** | | | |
| Softwood | 35.2 | 23.7 | 11.5 |
| Hardwood | 0.2 | 0.1 | 0.2 |
| Total | 35.4 | 23.8 | 11.7 |
| **Other industrial**[b] | | | |
| Softwood | 16.5 | 4.2 | 12.3 |
| Hardwood | 2.2 | — | 2.2 |
| Total | 18.7 | 4.2 | 14.5 |
| **Total industrial products** | | | |
| Softwood | 611.2 | 532.7 | 78.6 |
| Hardwood | 114.7 | 107.6 | 7.1 |
| Total | 726.0 | 640.3 | 85.7 |
| **Fuelwood**[c] | | | |
| Softwood | 3.6 | 3.3 | 0.3 |
| Hardwood | 25.4 | 25.0 | 0.4 |
| Total | 29.0 | 28.3 | 0.7 |
| **All products** | | | |
| Softwood | 614.9 | 536.0 | 78.9 |
| Hardwood | 140.1 | 132.6 | 7.5 |
| Total | 755.0 | 668.6 | 86.4 |

Numbers in rows and columns may not sum to totals due to rounding.
— = no sample for the cell; 0.0 = a value of > 0.0 but < 0.05 for the cell.

[a] Roundwood figures include an estimated 6.2 million cubic feet of roundwood chipped at other primary wood-using plants.

[b] Includes litter, mulch, particleboard, charcoal, and other specialty products.

[c] Excludes approximately 40.4 million cubic feet of wood residues and 48.7 million cubic feet of bark used for industrial fuel.

Figure 17 shows trends in average annual total product output from 1958 through 2005. While output used for saw logs and other industrial products were up slightly, roundwood used for veneer logs, pulpwood, and fuelwood were down from the previous survey period. The seven pulpmills operating in South Carolina between 2001 and 2005 made pulpwood the primary wood product produced during the latest survey period. Pulpwood output accounted for 49 percent of total product output for the State. With some minor fluctuations, this proportion has remained relatively constant over the last six survey periods (table 9). Pulpwood production was down nearly 6 percent, averaging just over 369 million cubic feet annually for the period. This decline was due to a 30-percent drop in hardwood pulpwood output.

Softwood pulpwood production totaled 290 million cubic feet—up 4 percent—and accounted for 78 percent of total pulpwood production, while hardwood pulpwood production amounted to 79.5 million cubic feet (table 8). Plant byproducts,

or mill residue, accounted for 18 and 6 percent, respectively, of total softwood and hardwood pulpwood production. The 58 million cubic feet of plant byproducts used for pulpwood production accounted for 33 percent of mill residue utilized for products.

Saw-log production used mainly for dimension lumber totaled just over 261 million cubic feet. Saw-log output from about 50 sawmills accounted for 35 percent of the total TPO volume between 2001 and 2005. Veneer-log production totaled 41 million cubic feet, while composite panel production amounted to 35 million cubic feet. Veneer and composite panel production combined accounted for 10 percent of the total product output. At 19 million cubic feet, other industrial products which includes poles, accounted for 2 percent of total product output. Industrial products accounted for 96 percent of the State's total product output. Domestic fuelwood totaled nearly 29 million cubic feet, and accounted for 4 percent of total product output for the State (table 8). Mill residue used for industrial fuel amounted to

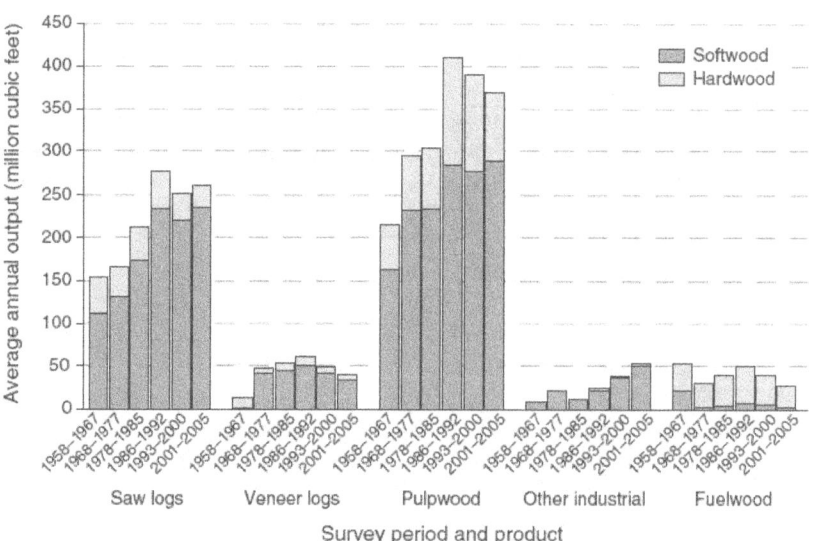

Figure 17—Average annual output of timber products by survey period, product, and species group, South Carolina, 1958 to 2005.

89 million cubic feet and accounted for 51 percent of the total mill byproducts utilized (table 10).

Average annual output of roundwood products (including domestic fuelwood) was down 1 percent, or 4 million cubic feet, to an average of 669 million cubic feet between 2001 and 2005 (table 11). Softwood roundwood production was up nearly 9 percent from 493 to 536 million cubic feet, while hardwood roundwood production declined 26 percent from 180 to 133 million cubic feet.

During the latest survey period roundwood harvested for saw log and pulpwood production amounted to 260 and 311 million cubic feet, respectively. These two products accounted for 85 percent of the total roundwood production for the State. Although average TPO volumes for the latest survey period show a slight decline, the most recent industry surveys indicate increasing product output due to industrial expansion (see fig. 13). With that increase, average TPO volume for the next survey period should capture the additional mill capacity.

For all products, 94 percent of the roundwood products volume came from growing-stock trees, split between sawtimber (70 percent) and poletimber (30 percent) (table 11). Volume from other sources, which includes premerchantable, rough cull and salvable dead trees, and stumps and tops of harvested trees, amounted to 38 million cubic feet. This volume accounted for 6 percent of total roundwood product output.

**Table 9—Output of timber products by product type, survey years, and species group, South Carolina**

| Product type and survey years | Softwood | Hardwood | Total | Proportion of total |
|---|---|---|---|---|
| | *thousand cubic feet* | | | |
| **Saw logs** | | | | |
| 1958 to 1967 | 111,572 | 42,838 | 154,410 | 0.35 |
| 1968 to 1977 | 131,975 | 33,714 | 165,689 | 0.29 |
| 1978 to 1985 | 172,852 | 40,011 | 212,863 | 0.34 |
| 1986 to 1992 | 233,400 | 43,500 | 276,900 | 0.33 |
| 1993 to 2000 | 221,038 | 31,598 | 252,636 | 0.33 |
| 2001 to 2005 | 235,592 | 25,626 | 261,218 | 0.35 |
| **Veneer logs** | | | | |
| 1958 to 1967 | 851 | 12,135 | 12,986 | 0.03 |
| 1968 to 1977 | 41,687 | 6,944 | 48,631 | 0.09 |
| 1978 to 1985 | 45,441 | 9,154 | 54,595 | 0.09 |
| 1986 to 1992 | 51,700 | 10,200 | 61,900 | 0.07 |
| 1993 to 2000 | 42,913 | 7,628 | 50,541 | 0.07 |
| 2001 to 2005 | 34,299 | 7,128 | 41,427 | 0.05 |
| **Pulpwood** | | | | |
| 1958 to 1967 | 163,599 | 52,803 | 216,402 | 0.48 |
| 1968 to 1977 | 232,955 | 63,400 | 296,355 | 0.53 |
| 1978 to 1985 | 234,472 | 70,228 | 304,700 | 0.49 |
| 1986 to 1992 | 284,500 | 126,300 | 410,800 | 0.50 |
| 1993 to 2000 | 278,295 | 112,841 | 391,136 | 0.50 |
| 2001 to 2005 | 289,630 | 79,516 | 369,146 | 0.49 |
| **Other industrial** | | | | |
| 1958 to 1967 | 9,182 | 629 | 9,811 | 0.02 |
| 1968 to 1977 | 22,310 | 214 | 22,524 | 0.04 |
| 1978 to 1985 | 12,100 | 596 | 12,696 | 0.02 |
| 1986 to 1992 | 22,600 | 3,400 | 26,000 | 0.03 |
| 1993 to 2000 | 37,239 | 2,706 | 39,945 | 0.05 |
| 2001 to 2005 | 51,727 | 2,434 | 54,161 | 0.07 |
| **Fuelwood** | | | | |
| 1958 to 1967 | 22,071 | 31,650 | 53,721 | 0.12 |
| 1968 to 1977 | 2,843 | 28,260 | 31,103 | 0.06 |
| 1978 to 1985 | 5,252 | 36,066 | 41,318 | 0.07 |
| 1986 to 1992 | 7,600 | 43,600 | 51,200 | 0.06 |
| 1993 to 2000 | 5,720 | 35,338 | 41,058 | 0.05 |
| 2001 to 2005 | 3,648 | 25,379 | 29,027 | 0.04 |
| **All products** | | | | |
| 1958 to 1967 | 307,275 | 140,055 | 447,330 | 1.00 |
| 1968 to 1977 | 431,770 | 132,532 | 564,302 | 1.00 |
| 1978 to 1985 | 470,117 | 156,055 | 626,172 | 1.00 |
| 1986 to 1992 | 599,800 | 227,000 | 826,800 | 1.00 |
| 1993 to 2000 | 585,205 | 190,111 | 775,316 | 1.00 |
| 2001 to 2005 | 614,896 | 140,083 | 754,979 | 1.00 |

**Table 10—Disposal of average annual volume of residue at primary wood-using plants by product, species group, and type of residue, South Carolina, 2001 to 2005**

| Product and species group | All types | Bark | Coarse[a] | Fine[b] |
|---|---|---|---|---|
| | | | *million cubic feet* | |
| **Fiber products** | | | | |
| Softwood | 53.1 | — | 47.7 | 5.4 |
| Hardwood | 4.8 | — | 4.8 | — |
| Total | 57.9 | — | 52.4 | 5.4 |
| **Particleboard** | | | | |
| Softwood | 11.5 | 0.0 | 2.0 | 9.5 |
| Hardwood | 0.2 | 0.0 | — | 0.2 |
| Total | 11.7 | 0.0 | 2.0 | 9.6 |
| **Sawn products** | | | | |
| Softwood | 1.6 | — | 1.6 | — |
| Hardwood | 0.0 | — | 0.0 | — |
| Total | 1.6 | — | 1.6 | — |
| **Industrial fuel** | | | | |
| Softwood | 72.0 | 37.9 | 5.0 | 29.0 |
| Hardwood | 17.1 | 10.7 | 1.2 | 5.2 |
| Total | 89.0 | 48.7 | 6.2 | 34.2 |
| **Domestic fuel** | | | | |
| Softwood | 0.3 | — | 0.3 | — |
| Hardwood | 0.4 | — | 0.4 | — |
| Total | 0.7 | — | 0.7 | — |
| **Miscellaneous** | | | | |
| Softwood | 2.3 | 6.5 | 0.6 | 5.2 |
| Hardwood | 2.2 | 1.5 | 0.2 | 0.5 |
| Total | 14.5 | 8.0 | 0.8 | 5.7 |
| **Not used** | | | | |
| Softwood | 0.2 | 0.1 | 0.0 | 0.1 |
| Hardwood | 0.1 | 0.0 | 0.1 | 0.0 |
| Total | 0.4 | 0.2 | 0.1 | 0.1 |
| **All products** | | | | |
| Softwood | 151.1 | 44.6 | 57.3 | 49.2 |
| Hardwood | 24.7 | 12.3 | 6.6 | 5.8 |
| Total | 175.8 | 56.8 | 63.9 | 55.0 |

Numbers in rows and columns may not sum to totals due to rounding.

— = no sample for the cell; 0.0 = a value of > 0.0 but < 0.05 for the cell.

[a] Material such as slabs and edgings.

[b] Material such as sawdust and shavings.

Table 11—Average annual output of roundwood products by product, species group, and source of material, South Carolina, 2001 to 2005

| Product and species group | All sources | Growing-stock trees[a] | | | Other sources[b] |
|---|---|---|---|---|---|
| | | Total | Sawtimber | Poletimber | |
| | | | *million cubic feet* | | |
| **Saw logs** | | | | | |
| Softwood | 234.0 | 226.3 | 211.8 | 14.5 | 7.7 |
| Hardwood | 25.6 | 25.1 | 23.6 | 1.5 | 0.5 |
| Total | 259.6 | 251.4 | 235.4 | 16.1 | 8.2 |
| **Veneer logs** | | | | | |
| Softwood | 34.3 | 33.5 | 33.0 | 0.5 | 0.8 |
| Hardwood | 7.1 | 7.0 | 7.0 | — | 0.1 |
| Total | 41.4 | 40.6 | 40.0 | 0.5 | 0.9 |
| **Pulpwood** | | | | | |
| Softwood | 236.5 | 219.9 | 101.4 | 118.5 | 16.6 |
| Hardwood | 74.8 | 69.3 | 29.8 | 39.6 | 5.4 |
| Total | 311.3 | 289.2 | 131.1 | 158.1 | 22.0 |
| **Composite panels** | | | | | |
| Softwood | 23.7 | 21.7 | 9.8 | 11.9 | 2.0 |
| Hardwood | 0.1 | 0.1 | 0.0 | 0.0 | 0.0 |
| Total | 23.8 | 21.8 | 9.8 | 11.9 | 2.0 |
| **Other industrial** | | | | | |
| Softwood | 4.2 | 3.8 | 3.7 | 0.1 | 0.4 |
| Hardwood | — | — | — | — | — |
| Total | 4.2 | 3.8 | 3.7 | 0.1 | 0.4 |
| **Total industrial products** | | | | | |
| Softwood | 532.7 | 505.2 | 359.7 | 145.5 | 27.4 |
| Hardwood | 107.6 | 101.6 | 60.4 | 41.2 | 6.0 |
| Total | 640.3 | 606.8 | 420.1 | 186.7 | 33.4 |
| **Fuelwood** | | | | | |
| Softwood | 3.3 | 1.3 | 0.7 | 0.6 | 2.1 |
| Hardwood | 25.0 | 22.7 | 18.1 | 4.6 | 2.3 |
| Total | 28.3 | 24.0 | 18.8 | 5.2 | 4.3 |
| **All products** | | | | | |
| Softwood | 536.0 | 506.5 | 360.4 | 146.1 | 29.5 |
| Hardwood | 132.6 | 124.3 | 78.6 | 45.7 | 8.3 |
| Total | 668.6 | 630.8 | 438.9 | 191.9 | 37.8 |

Numbers in rows and columns may not sum to totals due to rounding.

— = no sample for the cell; 0.0 = a value of > 0.0 but < 0.05 for the cell.

[a] On timberland.

[b] Includes trees < 5.0 inches in diameter, tree tops and limbs from timberland, or material from other forest land or nonforest land such as fence rows or suburban areas.

### Total Timber Removals: Products, Logging Residues, and Other Removals

Total timber removals encompasses more than volume utilized for timber products. Total timber removals, averaged over the time period, are the sum of the volume of roundwood products, logging residues (unused portions of trees left in the woods which includes volume from tops, limbs, and stumps), and other removals (removals attributed to land clearing or land use changes) from growing-stock and nongrowing-stock sources. Removals from all sources, for both softwoods and hardwoods combined, totaled 1.0 billion cubic feet over the 2001 to 2005 survey period (table 12). Roundwood products accounted for 67 percent of total removals. Logging residues and other removals amounted to 219 million cubic feet (22 percent) and 116 million cubic feet (11 percent) of total removals, respectively.

**Table 12—Volume of timber removals by removals class, species group, and source, South Carolina, 2001 to 2005**

| Removals class and species group | All sources | Source Growing stock | Nongrowing stock |
|---|---|---|---|
| | | *million cubic feet* | |
| **Roundwood products** | | | |
| Softwood | 536.0 | 506.5 | 29.5 |
| Hardwood | 132.6 | 124.3 | 8.3 |
| Total | 668.6 | 630.8 | 37.8 |
| **Logging residues** | | | |
| Softwood | 152.6 | 42.5 | 110.1 |
| Hardwood | 66.8 | 20.6 | 46.2 |
| Total | 219.4 | 63.1 | 156.3 |
| **Other removals** | | | |
| Softwood | 45.6 | 32.6 | 13.1 |
| Hardwood | 70.6 | 37.6 | 32.9 |
| Total | 116.2 | 70.2 | 46.0 |
| **Total removals** | | | |
| Softwood | 734.3 | 581.6 | 152.6 |
| Hardwood | 269.9 | 182.5 | 87.4 |
| Total | 1,004.2 | 764.1 | 240.0 |

Numbers in rows and columns may not sum to totals due to rounding.

Forestry is the #1 manufacturing industry in South Carolina in terms of jobs (44,708) and payroll ($2.4 billion).

## South Carolina's Forest Products Exports

The export of South Carolina forest products approached $1 billion in annual value in 2006 (South Carolina Forestry Commission 2007). Aided by the declining value of U.S. currency in the world market, the value of forest products exports grew 59 percent, from $604 million in 2001 to >$962 million in 2006 (fig. 18).

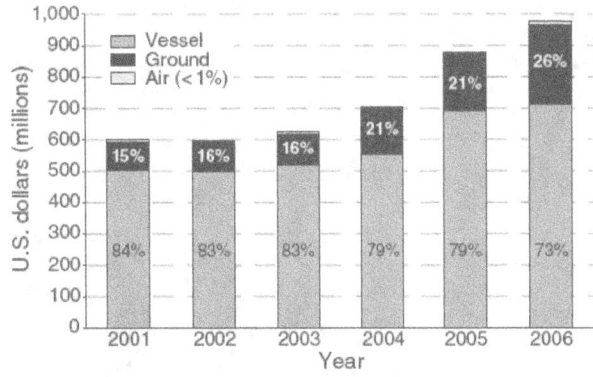

Figure 18—South Carolina forest products exports, 2001 to 2006.

Mill residues are in high demand as a source of fiber and biomass.

37

*Solid-wood products, such as these utility poles, account for almost one-fourth of forestry's total economic impact in South Carolina.*

The bulk of South Carolina's forest products leave the State via ocean-going vessels, but the importance of ground transportation has grown in recent years. Forest products are the most important commodity moved through the Port of Charleston, accounting for 27 percent of the total cargo volume in 2006. Besides ports, South Carolina offers well developed and extensive railway and highway systems.

### Export Markets

South Carolina forest products are in demand around the world. Overall, Canada is the leading export destination for South

Carolina forest products. Between 2001 and 2006, products worth $705 million left the State and crossed the Canadian border. Italy ($428 million), the Netherlands ($328 million), China ($298 million), and Germany ($231 million) complete the list of the top five export destinations. Each of these countries imported a record value of South Carolina forest products in 2006.

### Pulp and Paper Products

The pulp and paper industry accounts for 90 percent of the total forest products exported from South Carolina. Paper and paperboard are the State's leading forest product export,

accounting for $2.5 billion, or 58 percent, of the total exports between 2001 and 2006. Export of paper and paperboard-related products have experienced double-digit growth rates every year since 2003. The top five markets for paper and paperboard-related products are Canada, China, Italy, Germany, and Mexico.

Wood pulp product exports have also been very successful. Total export figures for the 6-year period were valued at $1.5 billion. Wood pulp exports have been up every year since 2001. Between 2005 and 2006, export of wood pulp increased $36 million. The top five markets for South Carolina wood pulp are the Netherlands, Italy, Germany, South Korea, and Japan.

## Wood Products

The export of solid wood products makes up 10 percent of the total forest product exports from South Carolina. Over the 6-year period, from 2001 to 2006, wood exports totaled $390 million. These wood exports range from unprocessed logs to primary wood products such as lumber and moldings. Lumber accounted for $207 million or 53 percent of the solid wood exports. The other segments of this category were fairly evenly distributed. Wood exports are well-diversified across many countries, with only Canada, Japan, and China accounting for double-digit export shares.

Wood furniture and pine oils added $47 million and $526,000, respectively, to South Carolina forest product exports between 2001 and 2006. As these export figures suggest, both categories play less significant roles in overall forest product exports. Main wood furniture export destinations were Japan, Panama, and Canada, while pine oil exports went largely to Costa Rica, Chile, and Jamaica.

Forest products are the leading commodity moved through the Port of Charleston. (photo courtesy of the Port of Charleston)

## Specialty Forest Products

Nontimber benefits of the forest such as specialty forest products, recreation, water, wildlife habitat, and aesthetic values also contribute greatly to the State's economy and well-being of the general population. Specialty forest products or nontimber forest products (NTFPs) have been harvested from South Carolina forests for many years. Although these products contribute a much smaller percentage to the overall economy than traditional forest products, they are very important and provide millions of dollars to many local rural economies each year. Many of these products are collected with very little forest disturbance and range from edible products (fruits, nuts, mushrooms, ramps, and maple syrup), to medicinal-type products (saw palmetto and bloodroot), to ornamental products (galax,

pine tips for garlands, and grapevines), landscape products (pine straw and native plants) and specialty woods (burl and crotch wood for fine crafts).

According to an April 2003 survey of county extension agents, South Carolina had a total of 556 NTFP enterprises (Chamberlain and Predny 2003). Table 13 shows the total number of NTFP enterprises Southwide. Fifty-three percent, or 297, of the NTFP enterprises in the State fell into the specialty wood and landscape categories. Medicinal plants and edible products comprised 114, or 21 percent, of the NTFP enterprises, while the floral and decorative products category had 145, or 26 percent, of the firms. South Carolina ranked 12th in total number of NTFP enterprises in the southern region, accounting for 2 percent of the total NTFP firms.

Table 13—Total number and distribution of nontimber forest product enterprises in the Southern United States as received by county extension agents

| State | Edible | Specialty wood | Floral and decorative | Landscape | Medicinal | Total |
|---|---|---|---|---|---|---|
| | | | number | | | |
| Alabama | 221 | 377 | 378 | 377 | 58 | 1,411 |
| Arkansas | 224 | 257 | 208 | 120 | 251 | 1,060 |
| Florida | 216 | 127 | 182 | 837 | 50 | 1,412 |
| Georgia | 250 | 186 | 384 | 1,086 | 68 | 1,974 |
| Kentucky | 490 | 826 | 562 | 373 | 2,670 | 4,921 |
| Louisiana | 249 | 119 | 94 | 81 | 8 | 551 |
| Mississippi | 234 | 252 | 207 | 192 | 15 | 900 |
| North Carolina | 526 | 452 | 3,283 | 1,326 | 770 | 6,357 |
| Oklahoma | 275 | 148 | 75 | 65 | 14 | 577 |
| **South Carolina** | **89** | **81** | **145** | **216** | **25** | **556** |
| Tennessee | 390 | 794 | 481 | 593 | 314 | 2,572 |
| Texas | 438 | 210 | 200 | 196 | 27 | 1,071 |
| Virginia | 239 | 370 | 698 | 376 | 262 | 1,945 |
| Total all States | 3,841 | 4,199 | 6,897 | 5,838 | 4,532 | 25,307 |

# Forest Health

Quantifying and assessing various aspects of forest health can be approached using a broad range of factors. Levels of tree mortality and determining what may have contributed to the trees' demise are important components of any assessment of forest health. Insects and disease are always present in forest environments, but it is only when widespread tree mortality occurs that their presence becomes a concern. Identifying which specific disease or insect is causing the mortality and determining whether it is native to the area or is an introduced species then becomes valuable. Estimating levels and cause of disturbance, and identifying the impacts from invasive plants also help quantify forest health.

## Tree Mortality

Total mortality on South Carolina's forest land averaged 199.6 million cubic feet per year between 2002 and 2006, totaling 998.0 million cubic feet for the period. Over one-half the mortality (56 percent) occurred on forest land owned by private individuals. The current level of mortality, while substantial, is nearly equal to the rate of loss reported between 1994 and 2001, indicating that forest health conditions are relatively stable.

Current mortality was split almost equally between softwood (54 percent) and hardwood (46 percent) species. The loblolly and shortleaf pine species group was the hardest hit of all softwoods, averaging 90.4 million cubic feet per year. Losses to other softwoods were minimal. For hardwood species, other red oaks species group averaged volume losses of 23.5 million cubic feet per year, followed by sweetgum where mortality claimed 17.2 million cubic feet annually.

Specific diseases or insects causing individual tree mortality are often difficult to determine. However, broad categories provide some information as to what might be the causal agent. In general, weather events—high winds or ice storms, for example—were the primary cause of death for all live trees, accounting for 27 percent of the mortality (fig. 19), followed by insects (21 percent ) and disease (19 percent). Vegetation (15 percent) as a cause of mortality includes tree death due to suppression (overtopping) or vines such as kudzu.

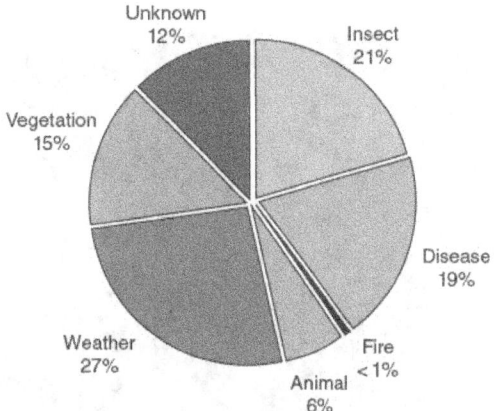

Figure 19—Annual mortality of live trees on timberland by cause of death, South Carolina, 2006.

### Redbay: Increasing Mortality Attributed to Laurel Wilt Disease

Redbay is a tree species common to the coastal regions of Texas to Virginia. Although not an important tree commercially, redbay fruit is a food source for many avian species, and tree foliage is a source of browse for deer and black bear (Johnson and others 2008). Recently, redbay mortality has been attributed to Laurel wilt disease. Redbay trees displaying symptoms of the disease have been detected in numerous counties of South Carolina, Georgia, and Florida (fig. 20). The disease—caused by a fungus (*Raffaelea* species)—is introduced into the tree by the ambrosia beetle (*Xyleborus glabratus*).

Experts estimate that the disease can spread unaided at about 20 miles per year. However, the rate of spread has been noted to be much higher because of human transport of infested wood. The fungus has also been shown to affect other tree species including sassafras and avocado. As yet, there are no known management strategies to prevent the spread or reduce the impact of the disease, short of burning or burying dead trees and avoiding transportation of diseased wood (U.S. Department of Agriculture 2008).

FIA surveys have not yet detected a substantial amount of mortality in redbay in South Carolina. As of the 2006 inventory, a few redbay trees dying due to disease have been noted in Orangeburg and Colleton Counties. There is no indication if Laurel wilt was the cause of death in these incidences of mortality. However, the disease apparently is spreading rapidly and redbay mortality may occur at rates high enough to be detected by FIA surveys in the near future. Close monitoring of FIA data will help track the spread of the disease and assess the impact it is having on redbay trees.

Symptoms of Laurel wilt disease on redbay. (photo by Laurie Reid)

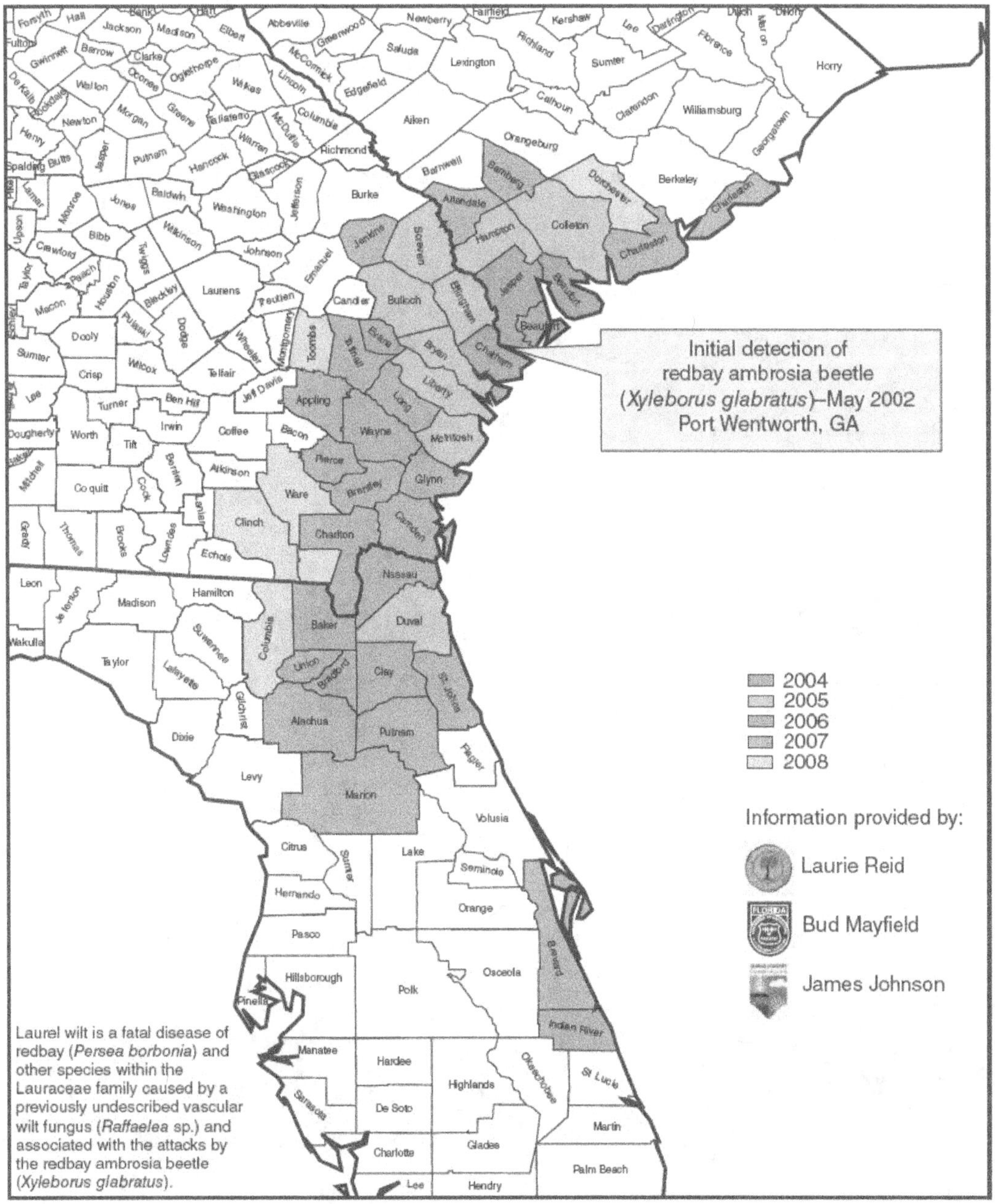

Initial detection of
redbay ambrosia beetle
(*Xyleborus glabratus*)–May 2002
Port Wentworth, GA

2004
2005
2006
2007
2008

Information provided by:

Laurie Reid

Bud Mayfield

James Johnson

Laurel wilt is a fatal disease of
redbay (*Persea borbonia*) and
other species within the
Lauraceae family caused by a
previously undescribed vascular
wilt fungus (*Raffaelea* sp.) and
associated with the attacks by
the redbay ambrosia beetle
(*Xyleborus glabratus*).

Figure 20—Distribution of counties with Laurel wilt disease symptoms, by year of initial detection
(Johnson and others 2008).

## Invasives

Invasive plant species are a continuing problem on forests in the South, and South Carolina's forests are no exception. Nor are they experiencing levels of invasives substantially above that of other Southern States. Invasive plants have the potential to change the ecological characteristics of a site, including modifying soil properties and out-competing native species. The overall result can include a reduced density and diversity in native woody regeneration (Oswalt and others 2007) which can impact the ecological and economic trajectories of forest stands. The data presented here were collected on 9,113 subplots between 2001 and 2006. Data are summarized by subplot.

Thirty-four percent (3,115) of all forested subplots sampled contained at least one nonnative invasive plant species. Japanese honeysuckle (*Lonicera japonica*) was the most frequently observed species, and occurred on 28 percent (2,555 subplots) of all forested subplots and 82 percent of all forested subplots containing at least one nonnative invasive species. Chinese/European privets were the second most common nonnative invasive species on sampled subplots. The most frequently observed nonnative invasive tree species was Chinese tallowtree (*Triadica sebifera*), which occurred on 55 forested subplots (2 percent). The distribution of the four most common nonnative invasive plant species detected on FIA sample plots is given in figure 21.

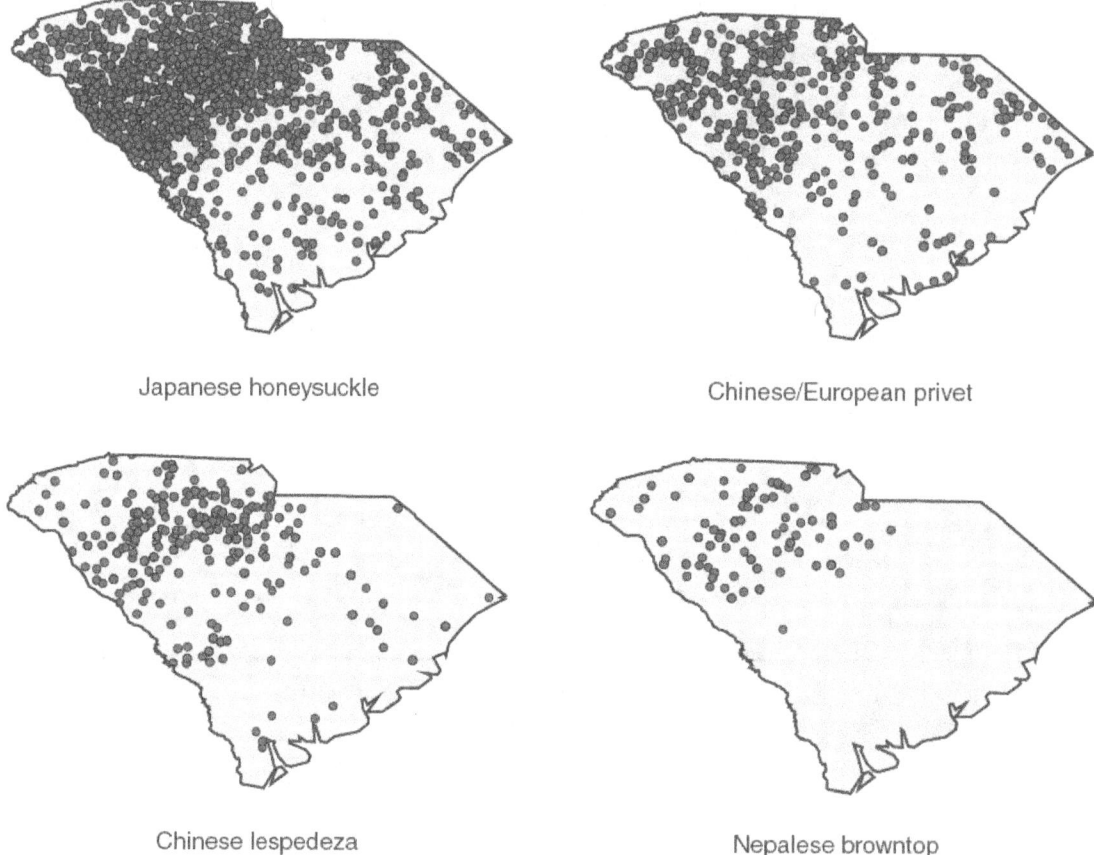

Japanese honeysuckle

Chinese/European privet

Chinese lespedeza

Nepalese browntop

Figure 21—Distribution of the four most common nonnative invasive plant species detected on Forest Inventory and Analysis sample plots, South Carolina, 2006.

## Summary

According to results from the 2006 FIA survey, there are 12.9 million acres of forest land in South Carolina, the high mark for estimates of forest land in the State. All indications are that these forested acres are relatively healthy (low mortality), and as productive today as they have ever been. Growth rates are at their highest reported levels and net growth substantially exceeds latest reported removals estimates. South Carolina boasts a surplus of wood volume available to meet future increases in demand for more wood products. Much of the surplus occurs on planted pine stands. This "wall of wood" has been amassing for years and is the result of landowner planting incentives offered in the mid-1980s. Similar incentives in the future will perhaps again be the key to maintaining South Carolina's wood volume at current record high levels.

Should an increase in demand arise, the State's forest resource stands ready to supply more raw material for wood products. With 72 percent of the total live volume in the hands of nonindustrial private landowners, the short-term question becomes one of incentive to harvest. Over the long term, significant reductions in recent planting rates are heightening concerns about the continued availability of an in-State supply of wood.

South Carolina's forest products industry is a primary component of the State's economy, contributing $17.45 billion annually. The State's 75 sawmills, pulpwood mills, and other primary wood-processing plants directly employed >21,000 individuals, with an annual payroll of $962 million. South Carolina forest products are in demand around the world as witnessed by record level exports in 2006 to Canada, Italy, the Netherlands, China, and Germany, and shipments to other countries, as well.

This analysis was based largely on results from the first complete remeasurement of the annual inventory locations established by the previous (2001) inventory. The SCFC-FIA data collection crews have already completed the first panel of the next (10th) inventory cycle. This new data will soon provide an updated estimate—a moving average—to timely track the extent and condition of South Carolina's forests. Unless results from this additional data drastically depart from recent trends, the expectation is for continued "good news" regarding the status of the State's forest resources.

Roll of paper is loaded into containers for shipping. (photo courtesy of the Port of Charleston)

## Literature Cited

Abt, K.L.; Winter, S.A.; Huggett, R.J., Jr. 2002. Local economic impacts of forests. In: Wear, D.N.; Greis, J.G., eds. Southern forest resource assessment. Gen. Tech. Rep. SRS–53. Asheville, NC: U.S. Department of Agriculture Forest Service, Southern Research Station: 239–268. Chapter 10.

Bechtold, W.A.; Patterson, P.L., eds. 2005. The enhanced Forest Inventory and Analysis program—national sampling design and estimation procedures. Gen. Tech. Rep. SRS–80. Asheville, NC: U.S. Department of Agriculture Forest Service, Southern Research Station. 85 p.

Butler, B.J. 2008. Family forest owners of the United States, 2006. Gen. Tech. Rep. NRS–GTR–27. Newtown Square, PA: U.S. Department of Agriculture Forest Service, Northern Research Station. 73 p.

Chamberlain, J.L.; Predny, M. 2003. Non-timber forest products enterprises in the South: perceived distribution and implications for sustainable forest management. In: Miller, J.E.; Midtbo, J.M., eds. Proceedings, first national symposium on sustainable natural resource-based alternative enterprises. Mississippi State, MS: Mississippi State University Extension Service and Mississippi State University Forest and Wildlife Research Center: 239–267.

Conner, R.C. 1998. South Carolina's forests, 1993. Resour. Bull. SRS–25. Asheville, NC: U.S. Department of Agriculture Forest Service, Southern Research Station. 78 p.

Conner, R.C.; Adams, T.; Butler, B. [and others]. 2004. The state of South Carolina's forests, 2001. Resour. Bull. SRS–96. Asheville, NC: U.S. Department of Agriculture Forest Service, Southern Research Station. 67 p.

Egbert, C.D.; Morris, J.A.; Nodine, S.K.; Straka, T.J. 1992. Forestry and South Carolina's forest resources—their economic importance. Circular No. 675. Clemson, SC: Clemson University, Cooperative Extension Service. 44 p.

Johnson, J.; Reid, L.; Mayfield, B. [and others]. 2008. New disease epidemic threatens redbay and other related species. http://www.state.sc.us/forest/idwilt.pdf. [Date accessed: June 17].

Johnson, T.G.; Harper, R.A.; Bozzo, M.J. 2004. South Carolina's timber industry—an assessment of timber product output and use, 2001. Resour. Bull. SRS–89. Asheville, NC: U.S. Department of Agriculture Forest Service, Southern Research Station. 33 p.

Johnson, T.G.; Knight, M. 2006. South Carolina's timber industry—an assessment of timber product output and use, 2003. Resour. Bull. SRS–106. Asheville, NC: U.S. Department of Agriculture Forest Service, Southern Research Station. 39 p.

Johnson, T.G.; Smith, N. 2007. South Carolina's timber industry—an assessment of timber product output and use, 2005. Resour. Bull. SRS–121. Asheville, NC: U.S. Department of Agriculture Forest Service, Southern Research Station. 28 p.

Knight, H.A.; McClure, J.P. 1979. South Carolina's forests. Resour. Bull. SE–51. Asheville, NC: U.S. Department of Agriculture Forest Service, Southeastern Forest Experiment Station. 66 p.

Little, E.L., Jr. 1979. Checklist of United States trees (native and naturalized). Agric. Handb. 541. Washington, DC: U.S. Department of Agriculture. 375 p.

Oswalt, C.M.; Oswalt, S.N.; Clatterbuck, W.K. 2007. Effects of *Microstegium vimineum* (Trin.) A. Camus on native woody species density and diversity in a productive mixed-hardwood forest in Tennessee. Forest Ecology and Management. 242: 727–732.

South Carolina Forestry Commission. 2008. IMPLAN analysis. Unpublished report. Available upon request from: South Carolina Forestry Commission, 5500 Broad River Road, Columbia, SC 29212.

South Carolina Forestry Commission. 2007. South Carolina forest products export 2001-2006. Columbia, SC: South Carolina Forestry Commission. 2 p.

Steel, R.G.D.; Torrie, J.H.; Dickey, D.A. 1997. Principles and procedures of statistics: A biometrical approach. 3$^{rd}$ ed. New York: McGraw-Hill. 666 p.

U.S. Department of Agriculture Forest Health Protection, Southern Region. 2008. Featured topics: Laurel wilt/redbay ambrosia beetle. http://www.fs.fed.us/r8/foresthealth/. [Date accessed: June 17].

U.S. Department of Agriculture Forest Service. 2004. Forest inventory and analysis national core field guide: field data collection procedures for phase 2 plots. Version 2.0. Washington, DC. 164 p. Vol I. Internal report. On file with: U.S. Department of Agriculture Forest Service, Forest Inventory and Analysis, 201 14$^{th}$ St., Washington, DC 20250.

U.S. Department of Commerce, Bureau of the Census. 1991. The 1990 decennial census. Washington, DC. [Not paged].

U.S. Department of Commerce, Bureau of the Census. 2000. The 2000 decennial census. Washington, DC. [Not paged].

U.S. Department of the Interior, U.S. Fish and Wildlife Service, and U.S. Department of Commerce, U.S. Census Bureau. 2007. 2006 national survey of fishing, hunting, and wildlife-associated recreation. FHW/06-NAT. 164 p.

## Glossary

Terms used in this report are defined in the Forest Inventory and Analysis glossary available on the FIA Web site (http://www.fia.fs.fed.us/tools-data/docs/). For a hardcopy of the glossary, please call 865-862-2000 or write to the following address:

Forest Inventory and Analysis
Southern Research Station
4700 Old Kingston Pike
Knoxville, TN 37919

Table Rock watershed in Pickens County.

## Summary of Data Tables

Tabular summaries of the 2006 survey data and data from previous inventories used in this report are available at http://srsfia2.fs.fed.us/states/south_carolina.shtml. Downloadable files and custom data tables for current and previous surveys are available at the FIA Mapmaker 3.0 Web site http://www.ncrs2.fs.fed.us/4801/fiadb/fim30/wcfim30.asp. A hardcopy of the 2006 inventory data summary tables is available by calling Forest Inventory and Analysis 865-862-2000 or writing to the above address.

Farm pond in Sumter County.

## Inventory Methods

The 2006 forest inventory of South Carolina was conducted by the Southern Research Station's Forest Inventory and Analysis (FIA) Unit in cooperation with the South Carolina Forestry Commission. This survey was the first remeasurement of data collection locations (plots) established in 2001 using the annual inventory methodology. The 2001 plots were distributed systematically across the State and estimates for area and volume were derived from measurements made at those locations. Growth, mortality, and removals estimates for the 2001 survey were derived from the remeasurement of trees on plots established by the 1993 periodic inventory. The 2006 survey marks the first time that the complete suite of forest resource estimates for South Carolina—area, volume, growth, mortality, and removals—are

based on plots established under a fully implemented annual inventory system.

In the current annual inventory system for the South, the objective is to measure about 20 percent (one-fifth) of the periodic inventory plot total across an entire State each year. This annual subsample is referred to as a panel. The plots that are measured in a single panel are selected to ensure systematic coverage of multicounty sampling units (fig. A.1). This systematic coverage includes forest and nonforest land. Estimates of forest characteristics can be derived using measurements from a single panel; however, the relatively small sample yields estimates with low precision. To achieve reliable statistics at the survey unit and State levels, panel datasets were combined using a moving average methodology. Estimates from plots that sampled forest land in all five panels were combined using the moving average procedure to produce the statistics in this bulletin.

### Data Comparisons— A Word of Caution

Users wishing to make rigorous comparisons of data between surveys should be aware of the differences in plot designs and variable assessments. Assuming there is no bias in plot selection or maintenance of plot integrity, the most valuable and powerful trend information comes from the same plots being revisited from one survey to the next and measured in the same way. This is also the only method that yields reliable components of change estimation (growth,

Figure A.1—Forest survey sample units, South Carolina.

removals, and mortality).
Consistency in sample
design lends a higher
level of confidence in
assessing trend, and
reduces variation that is
present in forest stands.
If sample designs change,
however, there is less
certainty in determining
if data trends are real or
are due to changes in
procedures. Even though
both sample designs may
be judged statistically valid,
the naturally occurring
variation in the data
from one plot design and
location to another hinders
rigorous assessments of
trend over time.

## Annual Sample Design: Three-Phase Sampling

The Southern Research
Station's FIA Unit uses
a three-phase sampling
method. Phase 1 (P1)
entails the use of National
Land Cover Data (NLCD)
to classify the land area
of each multicounty
survey unit into forest and
nonforest strata. Phase 2
(P2) and phase 3 (P3) are
based on a hexagonal grid
design that systematically
distributes data collection
locations across the State
(fig. A.2). In P2, data are
collected from a network of

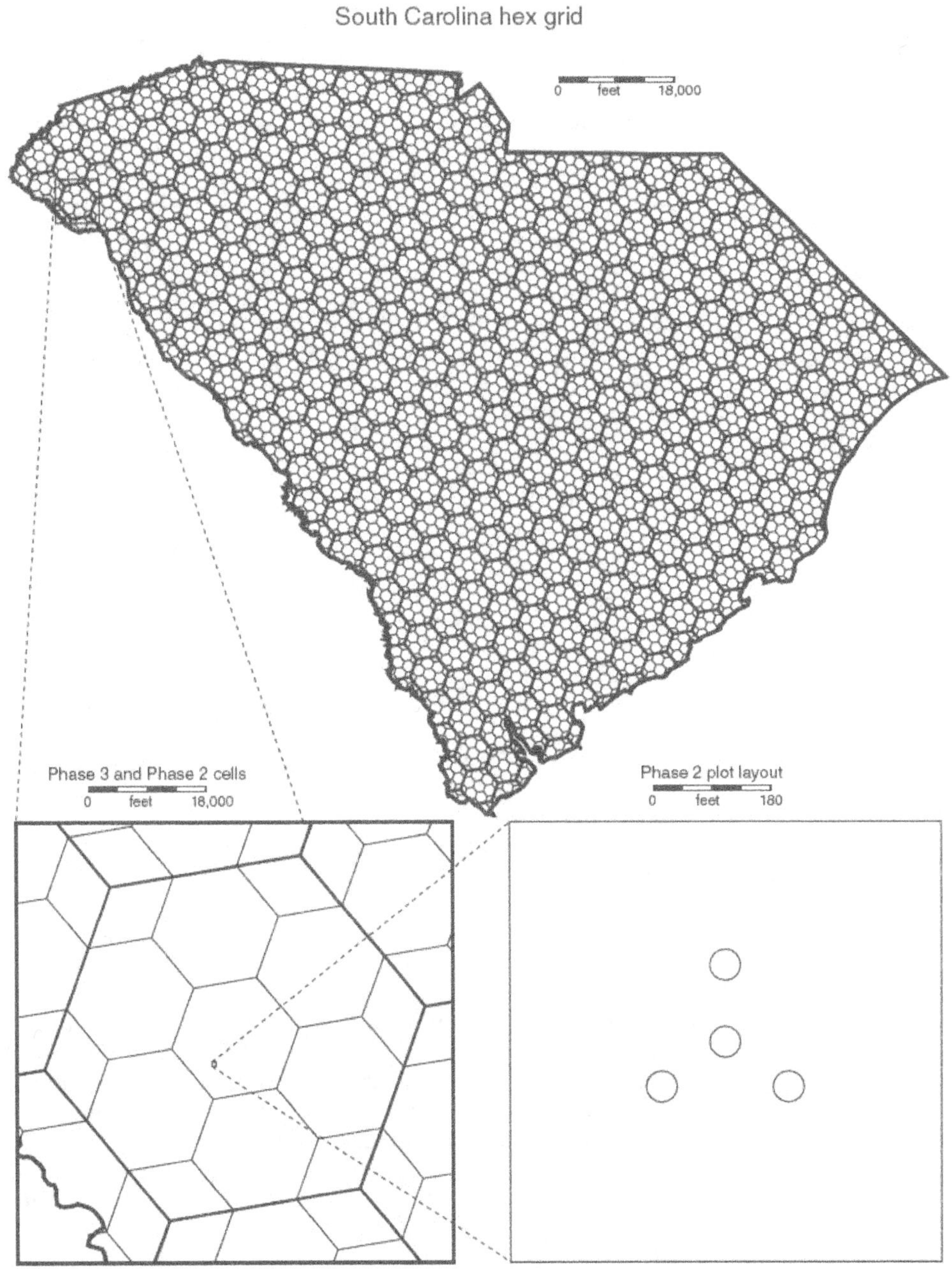

South Carolina hex grid

0    feet    18,000

Phase 3 and Phase 2 cells

0    feet    18,000

Phase 2 plot layout

0    feet    180

Figure A.2—Depiction of the FIA hexagonal grid system for the distribution of Phase 2 and 3 sample locations, South Carolina.

51

ground sample locations where field crews visit physical locations of plots and collect measurements of a variety of traditional mensurational FIA variables. Each P2 plot represents about 6,000 acres. P3 (forest health estimates) comprises a 1/16th sample of the P2 plots. P3 measurements include the full complement of traditional FIA variables measured on P2 plots, plus additional measurements taken to assess one or more of the following forest resource variables: tree crowns, soils, lichens, downed woody debris, and understory vegetation. Each P3 plot represents about 96,000 acres.

**Current phase 1—land area stratification**—P1 stratified estimation procedures reduce variance associated with estimates of forest land area and produce more precise estimates than simple random sampling. A statistical estimation technique is used to classify digital satellite imagery and initially stratify the land base as forest or nonforest to assign a representative acreage to each sample plot. Pixels within 60 m (2-pixel widths) of a forest/nonforest boundary formed two additional strata: forest edge and nonforest edge. Forest pixels within 60 m of the boundary on the forest side were classified as forest edge and pixels within 60 m of the boundary on the nonforest side were classified as nonforest edge. The estimated population total for a variable is the sum across all strata of the product of each stratum's area (from the pixel count) and the variable's mean per unit area (from plot measurements) for the stratum. Satellite imagery source data are from 2001 NLCD (30-m resolution). Recent aerial photography was used to select plots for measurement.

**Previous phase 1 methods**—For the 2001 inventory of South Carolina, the P1 forest area estimate was based on a grid of 25 points that was placed over the quadrant of an aerial photo where a P2 sample

plot was located. There were over 93,369 points, with each point representing about 220 acres. A photointerpreter classified each point as forest or nonforest and a percentage for each class was derived for each county. These photo classifications were adjusted based on ground observations at 5,629 sample locations. Forest area was then determined by multiplying the percentage of forested points by the U.S. Census Bureau's estimate of all land for each respective county (U.S. Department of Commerce 1991). Ground truths were done at each P2 sample location. Where a classification was found to be incorrect, a correction factor was calculated and the forest percentage that was derived from the original P1 point count estimate was adjusted. These correction factors adjust for possible misinterpretation of aerial photos and for real changes which may have occurred since the date of the aerial photography. Plot-level expansion factors were determined by dividing the number of forested plots into the total forest land.

**Phase 2—forest inventory**—The plot installed at each ground sample location P2 was comprised of a cluster of four points spaced 120 feet apart (Bechtold and Patterson 2005). Each point served as the center of a 1/24-acre circular subplot used to sample trees ≥ 5.0 inches in diameter at breast height (d.b.h.). A 1/300-acre microplot, offset from the subplot center, was used to sample trees 1.0 to 4.9 inches d.b.h. and seedlings (trees < 1.0 inch d.b.h.). These fixed-radius plots were established without regard to land use or land cover. At times, the cluster of four points straddles more than one land use or forest condition. Forest and nonforest condition classes were delineated and recorded on each plot. Condition classes were defined by six attributes: land use, forest type, stand origin, stand size, stand density, and major ownership class. The process of delineating

a fixed-radius plot into numerous sections based on forest and land use conditions is called mapping. All trees tallied were assigned to their respective condition class.

The cluster of four fixed plots sampled forest land at 2,483 ground sample locations in South Carolina. Current estimates of timber volume and forest classifications were derived from tree measurements and classifications made at these locations. Volumes for individual tally trees were computed using equations for each of the major species in South Carolina. Current estimates of growth, removals, and mortality were determined from the remeasurement of 1,834 permanent sample plots established by the previous annual inventory. For the 2006 survey, the net growth and removals estimates represent the average annual values for the period from 2002 to 2006.

**Phase 3—forest health**—Data on forest health variables P3 are collected on about 1/16$^{th}$ of the P2 sample plots. P3 data are

coarse descriptions, and are meant to be used as general indicators of overall forest health over large geographic areas. Forest health data collection includes variables pertaining to tree crown condition, down woody material (DWM), foliar ozone injury, lichen diversity, and soil composition. Tree crown health, DWM, and soil composition measurements are collected using the same plot design used during the P2 inventory data collection, while lichen data are collected within a 120-foot-radius circle around the center of each FIA P3 field plot.

Biomonitoring sites for ozone data collection are located independently of the FIA plot grid. Sites must be 1-acre fields or similar open areas adjacent to or surrounded by forest land, and must contain a minimum number of plants of at least two identified bioindicator species (U.S. Department of Agriculture Forest Service 2004). Plants are evaluated for ozone injury, and voucher specimens are submitted to a regional expert for verification of ozone-induced foliar injury.

FIA forester measures a large diameter pine in Darlington County.

53

## Reliability of the Data

A measure of reliability of inventory statistics is provided by sampling errors. Sampling error is associated with the natural and expected deviation of the sample from the true population mean. This deviation is susceptible to a mathematical evaluation of the probability of error. Sampling errors for State totals are based on one standard deviation, meaning that the chances are two out of three that the true population value is within the limits indicated by a confidence interval.

FIA inventories supported by the full complement of sample plots are designed to achieve reliable statistics at the survey unit and State levels. However, users should note that sampling error increases as the area considered decreases in magnitude. Sampling errors and associated confidence intervals are often unacceptably high for small components of the total resource.

Sampling errors (in percent) and associated confidence intervals around the sample estimates for timberland area, inventory volumes, and components of change are presented in the following tabulation:

| Item | Sample estimate and confidence interval | | Sampling error *percent* |
|---|---|---|---|
| Timberland (*1,000 acres*) | 12,800.6 ± | 52.5 | 0.41 |
| **All live (*million cubic feet[a]*)** | | | |
| Inventory | 21,487.9 ± | 369.6 | 1.72 |
| Net annual growth | 1,204.5 ± | 34.9 | 2.90 |
| Annual removals | 814.2 ± | 64.5 | 7.92 |
| Annual mortality | 198.1 ± | 16.1 | 8.13 |
| **Growing stock (*million cubic feet*)** | | | |
| Inventory | 19,162.5 ± | 344.9 | 1.80 |
| Net annual growth | 1,105.8 ± | 32.6 | 2.95 |
| Annual removals | 764.1 ± | 61.5 | 8.05 |
| Annual mortality | 161.5 ± | 15.2 | 9.39 |
| **Sawtimber (*million board feet[b]*)** | | | |
| Inventory | 66,476.3 ± | 1,648.6 | 2.48 |
| Net annual growth | 4,052.9 ± | 139.8 | 3.45 |
| Annual removals | 2,606.6 ± | 266.9 | 10.24 |
| Annual mortality | 477.0 ± | 58.2 | 12.21 |

[a] Includes palm species.
[b] International ¼-inch rule.

Statistical confidence may be computed for any subdivision of the State totals using the following formula. Sampling errors obtained from this method are only approximations of reliability because this process assumes constant variance across all subdivisions of totals.

$$SE_s = SE_t \frac{\sqrt{X_t}}{\sqrt{X_s}}$$

where

$SE_s$ = sampling error for subdivision of State total

$SE_t$ = sampling error for State total

$X_s$ = sum of values for the variable of interest (area or volume) for subdivision of State

$X_t$ = total area or volume for State

For example, the estimate of sampling error for softwood live-tree volume on nonindustrial private timberland is computed as:

$$SE_s = 1.72 \frac{\sqrt{21,487.9}}{\sqrt{7,467.6}} = 2.92$$

Thus, the sampling error is 2.92 percent, and the resulting confidence interval (two times out of three) for softwood live-tree inventory on nonindustrial private timberland is 7,467.6 ± 107.2 million cubic feet.

Planted longeaf pine on previous farmland in Sumter County.

**Table C.1—Common and scientific names of tree species tallied in South Carolina, 2006**

| Common name | Scientific name[a] | Common name | Scientific name[a] |
|---|---|---|---|
| Softwoods | | Hardwoods (continued) | |
| Southern redcedar | *Juniperus silicicola* | Hackberry | *C. occidentalis* |
| Eastern redcedar | *J. virginiana* | Eastern redbud | *Cercis canadensis* |
| Shortleaf pine | *Pinus echinata* | Flowering dogwood | *Cornus florida* |
| Slash pine | *P. elliottii* | Cockspur hawthorn | *Crataegus crus-galli* |
| Spruce pine | *P. glabra* | Downy hawthorn | *C. mollis* |
| Longleaf pine | *P. palustris* | Common persimmon | *Diospyros virginiana* |
| Pitch pine | *P. rigida* | American beech | *Fagus grandifolia* |
| Pond pine | *P. serotina* | White ash | *Fraxinus americana* |
| Eastern white pine | *P. strobus* | Carolina ash | *F. caroliniana* |
| Loblolly pine | *P. taeda* | Green ash | *F. pennsylvanica* |
| Virginia pine | *P. virginiana* | Waterlocust | *Gleditsia aquatica* |
| Baldcypress | *Taxodium distichum* | Honeylocust | *G. triacanthos* |
| Pondcypress | *T. distichum* var. *nutang* | Loblolly-bay | *Gordonia lasianthus* |
| Eastern hemlock | *Tsuga canadensis* | Carolina silverbell | *Halesia carolina* |
| Carolina hemlock | *T. caroliniana* | American holly | *Ilex opaca* |
| | | Black willow | *Juglans nigra* |
| Hardwoods | | Sweetgum | *Liquidambar styraciflua* |
| Florida maple | *Acer barbatum* | Yellow-poplar | *Liriodendron tulipifera* |
| Chalk maple | *A. leucoderme* | Cucumbertree | *Magnolia acuminata* |
| Boxelder | *A. negundo* | Mountain or Fraser magnolia | *M. fraseri* |
| Striped maple | *A. pensylvanicum* | Southern magnolia | *M. grandiflora* |
| Red maple | *A. rubrum* | Bigleaf magnolia | *M. macrophylla* |
| Sugar maple | *A. saccharum* | Sweetbay | *M. virginiana* |
| Yellow buckeye | *Aesculus octandra* | Southern crab apple | *Malus angustifolia* |
| Ailanthus | *Ailanthus altissima* | Chinaberry | *Melia azedarach* |
| Mimosa, silktree | *Albizia julibrissin* | White mulberry | *Morus alba* |
| Pawpaw | *Asimina triloba* | Red mulberry | *M. rubra* |
| Yellow birch | *Betula alleghaniensis* | Water tupelo | *Nyssa aquatica* |
| Sweet birch | *B. lenta* | Swamp tupelo, blackgum | *N. sylvatica* var. *biflora* |
| River birch | *B. nigra* | Eastern hophornbeam | *Ostrya virginiana* |
| American hornbeam, musclewood | *Carpinus caroliniana* | Sourwood | *Oxydendrum arboreum* |
| | | Redbay | *Persea borbonia* |
| Water hickory | *Carya aquatica* | Water-elm, planertree | *Planera aquatica* |
| Bitternut hickory | *C. cordiformis* | American sycamore | *Platanus occidentalis* |
| Pignut hickory | *C. glabra* | Eastern cottonwood | *Populus deltoides* |
| Pecan | *C. illinoensis* | Swamp cottonwood | *P. heterophylla* |
| Shellbark hickory | *C. laciniosa* | American plum | *Prunus americana* |
| Nutmeg hickory | *C. myristiciformis* | Black cherry | *P. serotina* |
| Red hickory | *C. ovalis* | White oak | *Quercus alba* |
| Shagbark hickory | *C. ovata* | Swamp white oak | *Q. bicolor* |
| Southern shagbark hickory | *C. ovata* var. *odorata* | Scarlet oak | *Q. coccinea* |
| Sand hickory | *C. pallida* | Southern red oak | *Q. falcata* |
| Mockernut hickory | *C. tomentosa* | Cherrybark oak | *Q. falcata* var. *pagodilolia* |
| Allegheny chinkapin | *Castanea pumila* | Scrub oak | *Q. ilicifolia* |
| Southern catalpa | *Catalpa bignonioides* | Bluejack oak | *Q. incana* |
| Sugarberry | *Celtis laevigata* | Turkey oak | *Q. laevis* |

*continued*

**Table C.1—Common and scientific names of tree species tallied in South Carolina, 2006 (continued)**

| Common name | Scientific name[a] | Common name | Scientific name[a] |
|---|---|---|---|
| Hardwoods (continued) | | Hardwoods (continued) | |
| Laurel oak | *Q. laurifolia* | Black oak | *Q. velutina* |
| Overcup oak | *Q. lyrata* | Virginia oak | *Q. virginiana* |
| Blackjack oak | *Q. marilandica* | Black locust | *Robinia pseudoacacia* |
| Swamp chestnut oak | *Q. michauxii* | Cabbage palmetto | *Sabal palmetto* |
| Chinkapin oak | *Q. muehlenbergii* | Weeping willow | *Salix babylonica* |
| Water oak | *Q. nigra* | Black willow | *S. nigra* |
| Oglethorpe oak | *Q. oglethorpensis* | Chinese tallowtree | *Sapium sebiferum* |
| Pin oak | *Q. palustris* | Sassafras | *Sassafras albidum* |
| Willow oak | *Q. phellos* | American mountain-ash | *Sorbus americana* |
| Dwarf chinkapin oak | *Q. prinoides* | American basswood | *Tilia americana* |
| Chestnut oak | *Q. prinus* | Carolina basswood | *T. caroliniana* |
| Northern red oak | *Q. rubra* | White basswood | *T. heterophylla* |
| Shumard oak | *Q. shumardii* | Winged elm | *Ulmus alata* |
| Post oak | *Q. stellata* | American elm | *U. americana* |
| Dwarf post oak | *Q. stellata* var. *margaretta* | Slippery elm | *U. rubra* |

[a] Little (1979).

Palmetto.

Conner, Roger C.; Adams, Tim O.; Johnson, Tony G.; Oswalt, Sonja N.
2009. South Carolina's forests, 2006. Resour. Bull. SRS–158. Asheville, NC: U.S.
Department of Agriculture Forest Service, Southern Research Station. 57 p.

Forest land area in South Carolina amounted to nearly 12.9 million acres, including 12.8 million acres of timberland. Nonindustrial private timberland totaled to 9.9 million acres. Family forest owners dominate the private ownership group with 262,000 landowners who collectively control 7.3 million acres of forest land in the State. Timberland area under forest industry ownership continued to decline, falling from just over 2.0 million acres in 2001 to 1.4 million acres in 2006. The loblolly-shortleaf pine forest-type group occupied 5.3 million of the 5.9 million acres of softwoods. Planted pine area amounted to nearly 3.1 million acres while area of natural pine totaled < 2.9 million acres. Hardwood forest types occupied 6.8 million acres of South Carolina's timberland, including 3.0 million acres of upland hardwoods. Total volume in all live species on timberland amounted to 21.5 billion cubic feet, surpassing all previous inventory estimates. All live softwood volume totaled 10.6 billion cubic feet with 8.8 billion cubic feet in the loblolly-shortleaf pine species group. Net growth for all live softwoods on timberland averaged 817.0 million cubic feet per year between 2002 and 2006. Annual removals of softwoods averaged 596.1 million cubic feet as of 2006, up 16 percent since 2001. Hardwood net growth averaged 387.3 million cubic feet per year since the 2001 survey while removals of hardwood averaged 217.7 million cubic feet per year. Forestry is a $17.45 billion dollar industry in South Carolina and employs nearly 45,000 people. Total output of timber products from the State's 75 sawmills, pulpwood mills, and other primary wood-processing plants averaged 755 million cubic feet per year between 2001 and 2005. Redbay trees displaying symptoms of Laurel wilt disease have been detected in numerous counties of South Carolina.

**Keywords:** Annual inventory, FIA, IMPLAN, National Woodland Owner Survey, pulpwood, timber product output, tree mortality.

The Forest Service, U.S. Department of Agriculture (USDA), is dedicated to the principle of multiple use management of the Nation's forest resources for sustained yields of wood, water, forage, wildlife, and recreation. Through forestry research, cooperation with the States and private forest owners, and management of the National Forests and National Grasslands, it strives—as directed by Congress—to provide increasingly greater service to a growing Nation.

**July 2009**

**Southern Research Station
200 W.T. Weaver Blvd.
Asheville, NC 28804**

South Carolina: The Palmetto State
Capital City: Columbia
Location: 34.03923 N, 080.88634 W
Origin of State's name: Named in honor of England's King Charles I
Population: 4 million
Geology: Land Area; 30,207 square miles
Highest Point: Sassafras Mountain; 3,560 feet
Inland water: 909 square miles
Largest City: Columbia
Lowest Point: Atlantic coast; sea level
Border States: Georgia - North Carolina
Coastline: 187 miles
Constitution: 8th State
Statehood: May 23, 1788

Bird: The Carolina wren is a member of the family Troglodytidae. It is present in all areas in South Carolina from the coast to the highest mountain. The song—which may be interpreted as tea-ket-tle, tea-ket-tle, tea-ket-tle, tea-ket-tle—may be heard the year-round, day and night, in all kinds of weather.

The Carolina wren is slightly smaller than an English sparrow and has a conspicuous white stripe over the eyes. The back of its body is rufous-red with underparts somewhat lighter in color. The tail, which is finely barred with black, is held erect when the bird is excited.

Agriculture: Tobacco, poultry, cattle, dairy products, soybeans, hogs.

Industry: Textile goods, chemical products, paper products, machinery, tourism.

Flag: Asked by the Revolutionary Council of Safety in the fall of 1775 to design a flag for the use of South Carolina troops, Col. William Moultrie chose a blue which matched the color of their uniforms and a crescent which reproduced the silver emblem worn on the front of their caps. The palmetto tree was added later.

Tree: Palmetto—Adopted as the "Official State Tree of the State of South Carolina" by Joint Resolution No. 63, approved March 17, 1939.

The South Carolina Palmetto is classified by the U. S. Department of Agriculture as "Inodes Palmetto (also called Sabal Palmetto) and commonly known as the Cabbage Palmetto." It has long been closely associated with the history of South Carolina, being represented on the State flag as well as on the State seal, where it is symbolical of the defeat of the British fleet by the fort, built of Palmetto logs, on Sullivan's Island.

The Palmetto is an attractive feature of the coastal areas of South Carolina and is also found in Georgia, Florida, and North Carolina. The large leafbud is highly prized as a salad vegetable for use in making pickles or relishes, and in Florida some use has been made of the fibers from the leaf bases. Such uses, however, are wasteful since the palm must be destroyed in either case and years must lapse before it can be replaced.

Flower: Carolina or Yellow Jessamine—Officially adopted by the General Assembly on February 1, 1924, for the following reasons: it is indigenous to every nook and corner of the State; it is the first premonitor of coming spring; its fragrance greets us first in the woodland and its delicate flower suggests the pureness of gold; its perpetual return out of the dead winter suggests the lesson of constancy in, loyalty to, and patriotism in the service of the State.

No flower that blooms holds such perfume,
As kindness and sympathy won.
Wherever there grows the sheltering pine
Is clinging a Yellow Jessamine vine.

(From "Legend of the Yellow Jessamine," by Mrs. Teresa Strickland of Anderson, SC)

The "Carolina or Yellow Jessamine" is defined by the New International Encyclopedia as "A climbing plant which grows upon trees and fences and bears a profusion of yellow, funnel-shaped flowers an inch in diameter, with a fragrance similar to that of the true Jasmine." Its odor on a damp evening or morning fills the atmosphere with a rare and delicate sweetness.

Mottoes: Animis opibusque parati (Prepared in mind and resources) — Dum spiro spero (While I breathe, I hope)

State information courtesy of www.50states.com